Satan's Devices

ROBERT MOREY

HARVEST HOUSE PUBLISHERS
EUGENE, OREGON 97402

SATAN'S DEVICES

Copyright © 1993 by Robert A. Morey
Published by Harvest House Publishers
Eugene, Oregon 97402

Library of Congress Cataloging-in-Publication Data

Morey, Robert A., 1946-
    Satan's devices / Robert Morey.
        p.   cm.
    ISBN 0-89081-881-9 — ISBN 1-56507-142-5
    1. Devil. 2. Spiritual warfare. I. Title.
BT981.M67   1993
235'.47—dc20   93-1132
                                                      CIP

Printed in the United States of America.

Special thanks to
New Life Bible Church
whose patience and love
made this book possible.

ABOUT THE AUTHOR

Dr. Morey is the Executive Director of the Research and Education Foundation and the author of over 20 books, some of which have been translated into French, German, Spanish, Italian, Finnish, Norwegian, Polish, and Chinese. He is an internationally recognized scholar in the field of comparative religions, the cults, and the occult.

Contents

Ignorance Is Not Bliss 7

Part I
The Basics

1. A Good Foundation 15
2. The Myth of the Comic Book Devil 23
3. Satan's Sure Defeat 35
4. A Classic Tale of Good and Evil 43
5. What's in a Name? 49
6. What Satan Can and Cannot Do 65
7. A Kingdom of Evil 85
8. Demon Possession 93
9. Setting Captives Free 105

Part II
Satan's Devices Against Christians

10. For All the Saints 115
11. Four Tested Strategies 129

Part III
Satan's Devices Against
Families, Churches, and the Nations

12. The Family Under Siege 145
13. The Gates of Hell 155
14. Disciple All Nations 167

Part IV
Satan's Devices
Against Non-Christians

15. Roadblocks 175

16. What About the Heathen? 181

17. Excuses, Excuses 193

    Suggested Reading 213

Ignorance
Is Not Bliss

For our struggle is not against flesh and blood, but against the rulers, against the powers, against the world forces of this darkness, against the spiritual forces of wickedness in the heavenly places (Ephesians 6:12).

One aspect of the Christian life that has been largely overlooked in modern times is the struggle believers face against the devices and schemes of the devil—devices which Satan uses to keep unbelievers from coming to Christ and Christians from living victoriously. Generations past were well informed about the devil. And it is no less essential to living a successful life in service to God and man today.

When was the last time you heard a sermon on the schemes of Satan? Have you been equipped to deal with the strategies Satan is using against your family and church at this very moment? Do you know how to defeat his evil plans for your children? Can you identify how he is trying to hurt your marriage?

The biblical record treats the devil as a sentient being who is a master criminal of great intelligence and malice. To underestimate his power and his schemes is to play the fool. But to overestimate his power is idolatry.

How can we fulfill the biblical mandate in Ephesians 6:11 to "stand firm against the schemes of the devil" if we are ignorant of those very schemes? How can we overcome the evil one as 1 John 2:13 urges if we have never given any attention to the nature and works of the demonic host?

A Life of Victory

The Bible presents the victorious life as one in which God by His sovereign grace enables us to persevere in holiness in the midst of and in spite of all our external trials and internal struggles:

> But now, thus says the LORD, your Creator, O Jacob, and He who formed you, O Israel, "Do not fear, for I have redeemed you; I have called you by name; you are Mine! When you pass through the waters, I will be with you; and through the rivers, they will not overflow you. When you walk through the fire, you will not be scorched, nor will the flame burn you. For I am the LORD your God" (Isaiah 43:1-3).

Instead of looking at the problems and difficulties of life as hindrances to holiness, the Bible sees these very same trials and struggles as part of the process of sanctification (Romans 8:28). Jesus did not pray to the Father to take us out of the world, to take us out of difficult situations, or even to deliver us out of the common trials which come to every person. Instead, He prayed, "I do not ask Thee to take them out of the world, but *to keep them from the evil one*" (John 17:15, emphasis added).

According to the Bible, the key to perseverance in the midst of trials is sound biblical knowledge. If we know God's Word, we will be able to walk through the trials of life and come out stronger and better for them. James writes, "Consider it all joy ... when you encounter various trials" (James 1:2).

Is this really possible? Yes! How and why can we do this? In verse 3, James tells us that the secret is in the *knowing*:

> Consider it all joy...when you encounter various trials, knowing that the testing of your faith produces endurance.

A knowledge of the ins and outs and the ups and downs of life is essential to maintaining a balanced Christian life. In other words, ignorance is not bliss when it comes to living the kind of Christian life God describes in His Word.

The apostle Paul put it this way in Romans 5:3: "We also exult in our tribulations, knowing that tribulation brings about perseverance."

Again, we can have joy in our tribulations because of something we know. If we know the purpose of our pain and suffering, then we can understand it. And if we understand it, then we can endure it with patience and joy.

God sends us trials in order to develop perseverance in us. And what does perseverance produce?

> Perseverance [brings about] proven character; and proven character [brings about] hope; and hope does not disappoint, because the love of God has been poured out within our hearts through the Holy Spirit who was given to us (Romans 5:4,5).

If we know that going through trials will develop godly character in us, then this hope does not disappoint us because God has poured out His love into our hearts by the Holy Spirit.

Throughout the New Testament, "knowing this" or "knowing that" was viewed as the basis of a successful

Christian life. Knowledge is the key that enables us to cope with everything that comes our way in life (Romans 5:3; 6:6,9; 13:11; 1 Corinthians 15:58; 2 Corinthians 4:14; 5:6,11; Galatians 2:16; Ephesians 6:8,9; Colossians 3:24; 4:1; 2 Timothy 2:23; Hebrews 10:34; 11:8; James 1:2,3; 3:1; 1 Peter 1:18; 5:9; 2 Peter 1:14; 3:17). This is especially true when it comes to understanding Satan's devices.

Doesn't Experience Count?

Many people struggle because they think they have to "feel" a certain way before they are living victoriously. Not once is "experiencing this" or "experiencing that" or "feeling this" or "feeling that" viewed as the basis of the Christian life. Knowledge, not emotionalism, is the key to winning in the midst of the trials and difficulties of life.

This is not to say that personal experience is worthless. Personal experience is never to be used as the source or basis of truth, but it can be used to *illustrate* truth. While God's Word must always be the basis of truth, we can call on our personal experiences to illustrate those truths we find in Scripture. So while personal experience can never "prove" the truth of a belief, it can be used to illustrate what we discover from the Bible.

What to Do When Trials Come

The moment you were born into God's family, did someone explain that you were going to have many trials in the Christian life? Or that your life may at times be harder than it was before you became a Christian? If not, they should have.

Jesus said, "In the world you [will] have tribulation" (John 16:33). The apostle Paul said, "All who desire to live godly in Christ Jesus will be persecuted" (2 Timothy 3:12). The book of Acts confirms that "through many tribulations we must enter the kingdom of God" (Acts 14:22).

The New Testament does not teach that the Christian life will be easy. It will often be extremely difficult.

Before you became a Christian, you floated like a dead fish on the fast-moving current of the world, the flesh, and the devil (Ephesians 2:1-3). Dead fish do not have to struggle to float downstream. All they have to do is give themselves up to the current. But once you become a believer, you will find that you have to swim upriver against the currents. These currents are flowing toward evil, not good. There are dangerous whirlpools, surges, and tides. Sometimes a current is stronger and sometimes it is weaker. But its pull toward evil is always the same.

Many Christians are never taught this realistic view of life. They are given the idea that everything will be wonderful because they are now saved. Supposedly, they will never have any more problems with spouses or children. They will never have any financial trouble or be tempted to sin. All their problems will be solved immediately and quickly by the Lord Jesus.

Well, obviously, these are only half-truths. The whole truth is that as Christians we can expect troubles within and without. As long as we are in this world, we will struggle against the world, the flesh, and the devil (Romans 7:14-25).

While we will experience more joy in the Christian life than sorrow, more pleasure than pain, there will be those times when we fall prey to the devices of Satan. We must be prepared for this. We must know how to duel with the devil and win.

To live right we must first know right. Then we can live the kind of life that pleases God.

PART I

The Basics

1

A Good Foundation

Two goals comprise the sum and substance of all the wiles of the devil. First, Satan wants to keep sinners from hearing the gospel. Or, if they hear it, to keep them from responding to it in faith. Second, once someone has become a child of God, Satan will try to make that Christian discouraged, bitter, sad, defeated, and depressed. He knows he cannot snatch that person's soul back, so he will do his best to make a believer's life ineffective.

When Christians become angry, bitter, and complaining, Satan can use them as excellent examples of why an unbeliever should *not* become a Christian. Non-Christians often say, "You want me to be saved? Look at old sourpuss Harry over there. If he's a Christian, I don't want to become one."

Satan will try to make us ineffective in the Christian life by reducing us to a depressed and discouraged state. And, sad to say, we fall into Satan's snares and traps all too often. He catches us in his web much too easily.

From the beginning we must understand that Satan has his favorite devices, schemes, plans, and methods of dealing with Christians, just as in our worst moments we have our favorite methods for getting our way. Many of Satan's devices have proved successful over thousands of years. Let's look back at some of the tricks he used with people in the church at Corinth.

Fingerprints of the Devil

The Christians at Corinth had fallen into the sins of gossip, slander, divisiveness, bitterness, and immorality. There was a noticeable lack of church discipline (2 Corinthians 12:20,21). The apostle Paul wrote two tough letters in which he dealt with the problems he saw in that church.

Paul demanded that church discipline be exercised on a man who was sexually involved with his stepmother (1 Corinthians 5:1-8). After the man was disciplined, he repented and wanted to be forgiven for what he had done. But some people would not forgive him. In his second letter, Paul urged all of the Corinthian Christians to forgive the man: "But whom you forgive anything, I forgive also; for indeed what I have forgiven, if I have forgiven anything, I did it for your sakes in the presence of Christ" (2 Corinthians 2:10).

The reason the Corinthians needed to forgive the man is found in verse 11: "in order that no advantage be taken of us by Satan; for we are not ignorant of his schemes." Paul viewed a festering spirit of bitterness and unforgiveness as a device Satan could use to cause division in the church. To him it was not just "one of those things" that happens in life over which we have no control. We have to keep reminding ourselves that we are not wrestling with flesh and blood, but against principalities and powers, against unseen wickedness in high places (Ephesians 6:10-19).

We tend to think that church problems are always caused by people. While it is true that rebellious people can be used, Paul identifies the real culprit behind the problems at Corinth: the prince of darkness. Not to forgive others is one of the tricks the devil uses to tear churches and personal relationships apart.

Paul clearly saw the fingerprints of the devil all over this situation. What was happening at Corinth was a scheme Satan was using to keep God's people in a depressed and discouraged condition and to nullify their witness to the world.

It is amazing that the early Christians were taught to recognize and defeat the schemes of Satan, but many Christians today are largely ignorant of his schemes. I don't remember ever being instructed by any pastor about the devices, schemes, and methods of Satan. No one told me that Satan has found certain methods that worked in the past and that he will no doubt try on me.

For much of the recent past, people who talked openly about the devil and his ways were quite extreme. They saw demons everywhere. If the car did not work, it had a demon in it. If they got sick, a demon was making them sick. They even claimed that Christians could be demon possessed!

Personally, I have no desire to come down with a bad case of "demonitis." I have no intention of seeing demons under every bed or running around casting demons out of everyone I meet. But I do believe we need to learn about the schemes of the devil. I believe we need a balanced approach to the devil and his ways that is edifying to the whole body of Christ (1 Corinthians 14:26).

At the end of a conference message I had given, a very distraught woman approached me and told me that in order to make some extra money she played the organ for another church on Wednesday nights. In that church the pastor and the people were continually casting demons out of each other. Although she herself had never joined in this, they had all gathered around her one night to cast a demon out of her! She didn't know how to respond.

I told her that God's Word does not teach that Christians can be demon possessed. There is not a single verse in the Bible which speaks of a demon-possessed Christian. Instead, when a person is in Christ, there is no communion between light and darkness (2 Corinthians 6:14). I suggested that she find other employment.

There is so much confusion and false teaching concerning the person, power, and ways of Satan today that we must stop and consider once again exactly what the Bible has to say on the subject. Above all, we must let the Bible interpret experience and not let experience interpret the Bible.

The Value of Understanding

The wonderful thing is that every Christian can know what the Bible says about the person and work of Satan. We can know who he is, what he is, why he is, where he is, what he does, what he can do, what he cannot do, and what his programs, plans, methods, schemes, and tactics are.

All of God's Word is valuable and profitable to the child of God (2 Timothy 3:15-17). Since God has chosen to reveal information about the person and work of the devil to us, it is our responsibility and our privilege to understand what He has revealed (Deuteronomy 29:29). Obtaining a biblical understanding of Satan and his ways will bring many positive results in the life of the Christian. Here are seven.

Seven Reasons to Understand Satan's Strategies

A biblical understanding of Satan will remove our ignorance. Ignorance is not bliss when it comes to the

Word of God. When Jesus rebuked the people of His own day for not knowing the Scriptures (Matthew 22:29), He was following the example of the prophets before Him (Hosea 4:6). Later the apostle Paul urged the Corinthians not to be ignorant of Satan or his schemes (2 Corinthians 2:11).

It will help us to avoid false ideas about him. There are a lot of fanciful ideas about the devil making the rounds these days. At one end of the spectrum are the people who see demons behind every bush. But at the other end of the spectrum are those who think the devil is a figment of overzealous imaginations. Having a balanced view of the devil will help us avoid dangerous extremes that lead to error.

It will release us from fear. All of us have fears. Some people fear poverty, old age, or sickness. Others fear the devil and his demons. Fear feeds on the darkness of ignorance, but it withers in the light of knowledge. As you begin to grow in your understanding of the nature of Satan and his work, including the limits of his power, your unhealthy fear of him will decrease.

It will keep us from worshiping the devil. Another reason not to be ignorant of the schemes of the devil is that fear can be a form of worship.

Several years ago, a woman who had been a missionary in Mexico was brought to my home. She had fallen into moral impurity and afterward went with some other missionaries to visit a demon-possessed man. When the demon was exorcised out of the man, it went into her. (Evidently, she was not a Christian or this could not have happened.) In any event, she ended up on my doorstep.

I went with her to a counseling center in Philadelphia run by a former seminary professor whom I trusted. After a great deal of sharing, we discovered that this woman was more afraid of Satan than she was of God.

Her fear of the devil was the chain which kept her in bondage to him.

When we tried to help her face the fact that she was more afraid of the devil than she was of God, she ran away. We never saw her again.

In Luke 12:5, Jesus says that we should not fear the devil because he can kill the body, but he cannot kill the soul. Instead, we should fear God because He can throw both the body and soul into hell. Jesus was making the point that our fear of God is to be stronger than our fear of Satan. The controlling factors in your life should be the smiles and frowns of God, not those of the devil.

While we should not fear Satan or his demons, we should have a healthy respect for their dangerous powers. Believers in Christ who would fight with the devil must have their armor on (Ephesians 6:10-20). Or as Walter Martin used to say, "He who would eat with the devil must have a long fork."

• *It will familiarize us with his favorite methods.* If Satan were to write a book on the psychology of the human species, we would be amazed. Satan is an astute observer of human nature. He knows how to attack us at the weakest point of our personality. He has certain methods he uses repeatedly for the simple reason that they are effective.

It will enable us to recognize and defeat his schemes. Let's use a simple illustration. Do you find yourself tempted to get angry week after week when it is time to leave for church and your kids cannot find their shoes? For you this may be something Satan uses to put you in such a foul mood that you cannot worship God or listen to the sermon.

If you understand that this is a device that Satan uses effectively in your life, you can counter his attack by laying out the clothes and shoes your children will need the night before. Set the table Saturday night for breakfast Sunday morning. Do whatever needs to be done to short-circuit the devil's plans and make Sunday morning more pleasant for everyone.

√ *It will keep us from false assurance.* Ignorance of Satan can be deadly. You may have accepted Christ as Lord, but what about your spouse or children? Don't you think that Satan has some ideas about how to seduce your children into sin? If you cannot detect or defeat his devices, how can you teach them to overcome his strategies?

Parents are more susceptible to this particular device of the enemy than almost anyone else. They often assure their children that they are saved when all the evidence is to the contrary. The book of 1 John warns us that if someone claims to be a Christian but "does not keep His commandments, [he] is a liar, and the truth is not in him" (1 John 2:4).

As parents we know how much we want our children to be saved. We pray and cry for their salvation. But we must not give them false assurance that might doom them.

A couple came to see me about their rebellious son. After hearing what their son was involved in, I offered the opinion that their son was probably not saved. The mother dogmatically stated that her son was indeed saved although he no longer believed in God and was heavily into drugs and sex! Her eyes flashed with anger at my suggestion that her son was not a Christian.

Her anger was misplaced. She should have been angry at herself. Not only had she herself fallen prey to one of Satan's devices, but she was also giving her son false assurance that could jeopardize him for eternity. Such assurance lulls children into a false sense of security, which the enemy uses to convince them that it does not matter how wicked they become, they are still "saved" because their mom says so.

While casting doubt on the salvation of this particular woman's son would not have "un-saved" him, giving him false assurance may well damn him. It would have been far better to tell him the truth.

She did not take my words well, complaining that if she gave up her assurance that her son was saved she could not sleep at night for worrying over him. What if he died and went to hell?

This is the real reason she and many parents like her hang onto the idea that their children are saved when they are far from God. These parents are concerned for their own peace of mind. They cannot handle the thought of their rebellious children dying that night from a drug overdose or car accident and ending up in hell.

The biblical antidote to the satanic device of giving false assurance to your children or anyone else is to understand that the Bible provides standards by which we can test someone's profession of faith to see if it is valid. Your children will not lose their salvation if you cast doubt on it. While such doubts have never damned anyone, presumption has damned millions.

The entire book of 1 John lays out the tests by which we can know if we or other people have eternal life. Just as "all that glitters is not gold," the fact that someone claims to be a child of God does not mean that he or she is. A biblical understanding of Satan and his ways will keep us from giving people false assurance and will stimulate our desire to witness for Christ.

2

The Myth of the Comic Book Devil

My daughter and I were watching a Woody Woodpecker cartoon one day when a leprechaun showed up at Woody's shack and offered him three wishes. He got the poor woodpecker into all sorts of trouble as he tried to teach Woody that you cannot get something for nothing.

Finally Woody was down to one wish, and his wish was that the leprechaun would go to hell. The floor opened up and the leprechaun slid down a long tube that ended in a cavern filled with flames.

The devil was pictured as a man with a pointed tail, horns, red suit, and a pitchfork. He said to the leprechaun, "Aha! So you are back?" He then proceeded to torment the leprechaun.

It's hard to imagine that anyone in our culture has escaped having this colorful impression of Satan made on his or her mind by countless comic books, cartoons, and movies. And since most churches never deal with the subject of Satan, this is the only picture that comes to mind when his name is mentioned. But this is not who the Bible is talking about when it refers to Satan.

Ripe for the Picking

Perhaps Satan's most successful device is to lure people into thinking that he does not really exist. Even people who claim to be Christians will say, "Satan does not really exist. You don't really believe in the devil, do you? He's just a childish fear." Or if they went to college, they might say, "Satan is only the projection of man's fear of the unknown which has been personified in various mythological figures."

This is why some professing Christians see little harm in watching demonic movies such as *Damien* or *The Exorcist.* They have fallen into a favorite device of Satan, which is having too *low* a view of him. It never occurs to them that the best trick Satan could use to defeat people is to get them to think that he does not exist. Then they are ripe for the picking.

There are many people today, including researchers and scientists, who are dabbling in what they call "psychic phenomenon." When the search for the "paranormal" first began, these people assumed that whatever or whoever they contacted on the "other side" would be good and kind. But as time has gone on they have had to admit that they are running up against what they call "evil vibrations."

They sometimes call these entities "poltergeists," which is a German word for a spirit that causes a lot of trouble. A poltergeist may do such things as throw dishes, pots, and pans around the kitchen, scratch the arms and faces of people, open and shut dresser drawers, pull the dog's tail, throw stones against the side of the house, etc. A poltergeist is decidedly not someone or something you would want as a houseguest.

People involved in ESP and psychic phenomenon are beginning to worry because they have tapped into something which they must admit is "evil." Yet they do not want to admit that the devil or his demons might exist.

Despite the Ph.D.'s following their names, most parapsychologists assume that the "devil" is the comic book figure in the red union suit. They cannot even consider the possibility that what they are dealing with is demonic or the devil because they have too low a view of Satan.

According to the Bible, the devil does not have horns, a pointed tail, or a pitchfork. He doesn't wear a red suit and run around hell tormenting people.

If someone asks you, "Do you believe in the devil?" it would be wise not to answer until they define what they mean by the word *devil*. If they mean the comic book devil, tell them, "No, I do not believe that such a creature exists. He is the invention of cartoon artists who let their imaginations get the best of them."

The Bible gives us a totally different view of the devil. Let me share with you what Scripture has to say.

The Real Satan

The Scriptures tell us that Satan is a finite spirit-being (that is, he is limited in his abilities), created by God at the dawn of history. We should actually refer to Satan as an "it" instead of a "he" because Satan is not a human male. Since spirit creatures do not have material bodies, they cannot be male and female. The Bible is clearly using anthropomorphic language when it describes the devil as a "he."

We speak anthropomorphically when we describe nonhuman things by attributing human qualities to them. For example, some people refer to their car or boat as a "she" and give it a woman's name. Many people talk about their computer in terms of "Well, he's acting up today." This is what we mean when we use the word *anthropomorphic*.

In addition, artists have long pictured women angels and cherubic baby angels, but there is no scriptural evidence for this. Whenever an angel takes on a visible form in Scripture, it is always that of a young man (Genesis 19, Luke 24:4, Acts 1:10, etc.).

I once mentioned that women angels are never mentioned in the Bible on a radio program. A caller brought up Zechariah 5:9, which speaks of two women with stork wings. However, according to all the classic commentaries on Zechariah, these winged women were symbols of evil. Also, they are not said to be "angels" in the text; rather, they are only part of a symbolic passage.

When medieval artists depicted angels as fat babies with wings on their backs and a bow and arrows in their hands, they were actually borrowing from the "cupid" of Greek paganism and not from the Bible.

According to the Bible, Satan is a fallen angel or spirit-being (Ephesians 2:2). Angels are not people and, despite many fables, when people die they do not become angels and get a pair of wings, a harp, and a cloud to sit on.

A Modern Definition

Since so many people today have a hard time understanding what an "angel" or "spirit" is, I have tried to find modern words and concepts by which to express old biblical truth to modern people. One way that seems to work well is to describe the devil as "an evil, alien, supradimensional energy-being composed only of mind or mental energy."

The word *supradimensional* simply means the devil can pop in and out of both the material and spiritual dimension. The word *energy-being* simply means that he is a spirit and hence he does not have a body (Luke 24:39).

The material universe can be perceived by man's five senses, but we cannot see, touch, smell, hear, or feel the devil because there is another world or dimension beyond the material world. Satan and his demons are composed of nonmaterial energy and can move from the dimension of the spirit to the dimension of matter.

The devil and his demons are not life forms native to this planet. They are invaders. They came here after they were kicked out of heaven. They are evil, nonmaterial beings who do not have physical bodies that can be seen or touched by man (except in certain situations). This is what I mean when I define them as "evil, alien, supradimensional energy-beings composed only of mind or mental energy."

No Match for God

Because Satan is only a created, finite spirit-being, he is not to be viewed as being equal to God in any sense.

Once again, we are faced with a popular misconception of the devil. Many people think that God and the devil are both eternal and equal in knowledge and power. This idea actually comes from the ancient pagan-occultic religion of Zoroastrianism.

Zoroastrianism taught that good and evil were eternal principles and that they were equal in power. This philosophy is sometimes called dualism, signifying that the principles of good and evil are the only two eternal realities.

Dualism can be refuted by pointing out that the idea that good and evil are two eternal principles is illogical because we can't call "x" good and "y" evil unless we have a third, higher standard which enables us to discern good *from* evil.

But then this third element must also be contrasted with something else and requires yet another higher standard, and this would go on ad infinitum. Dualism is internally self-contradictive and therefore destroys itself. (If you are interested, one of the best refutations of dualism was written by C.S. Lewis in his book *Mere Christianity*.)

While many people, even Christians, assume Satan is equal to God, this is not what the Bible teaches. Here are five proofs that Satan is not equal to God.

Satan Has a Beginning

Because Satan was created by God, he had a definite beginning and is therefore not eternal. He is merely a finite creature, and we should not ascribe any infinite attributes to him.

He Is Not Everywhere

The devil is not omnipresent. He cannot be everywhere at the same moment but only one place at one time.

If the devil is in my house attacking me at this moment, he cannot be in your house attacking you at the same time! The devil himself probably only deals with those people that he considers very important. It is not surprising then that Martin Luther, who relit the gospel light in the midst of nearly a thousand years of darkness and paganism in the Roman Catholic Church, relates having experienced personal attacks from the devil.

Thankfully, it is very doubtful that you or I will ever meet Satan himself. He may send one or more of his demons to attack us, but he cannot be everywhere at once. This is why we should hesitate to claim that "the devil made me do it." While a demon may have attacked us, *the* devil, Satan himself, was probably never anywhere near us.

We must also stop blaming the devil for the corruptions of our own hearts. Our problems are usually of our own making. This is why the book of James does not trace our temptations and sin back to Satan but to our own lusts (James 1:13-15). We give the devil far more credit than he deserves.

He Does Not Know All

• It is also helpful to know that the devil is not omniscient; he does not know all things. For example, he does not know what we are doing right now unless he happens to be in the same room with us. Neither does he know the future.

Because he is not omniscient, he makes plenty of mistakes. That is why those involved in the occult make false predictions. Satan can tell them what he is planning to do, but because God in His sovereignty often thwarts his designs, many of his plans and predictions do not come true.

If Satan knew the future, the occultists would be 100 percent accurate in their predictions. But they have only about the same success rate as one would gain from tossing a coin into the air.

He Is Not All Powerful

Satan is not omnipotent. He is limited in what he can do. He is a creature like you and like me, and he can only do those things which are consistent with his nature as an angel. We will talk about his nature more later.

He Is Invisible—Usually

As a spirit-being, Satan is normally invisible. Being composed only of spirit or mind, Satan is undetectable by the five senses. Thus in Luke 22:3 it says that Satan entered into Judas, yet no one saw it happen.

At the same time, Satan has the ability to appear in various forms just like any other angel. Angels can make themselves visible to the human eye and even produce a physical body which can be touched. For example, the two angels that went into Sodom to deliver Lot and his family could be seen and touched (Genesis 19:1,10,16). And throughout the New Testament, angels manifested physical bodies that could be seen (Matthew 28:2,3,5-7; Luke 1:11-20; John 20:12).

In this same way, Satan and his demons can at times be seen and touched. In the occult, these physical appearances are called "ectoplasmic manifestations or materializations." These spirit manifestations are, for all apparent purposes, material in nature. If you went up and hit one of them with your hand, your hand would hurt. This is not just smoke and mirrors. Although not their natural state, demons may materialize physically in various forms on a temporary basis.

Satan can appear in animal as well as in human forms. The snakes, bats, goats, dragons, etc., worshiped in pagan and occultic religions probably came from some satanic materialization in the past. Hence the biblical view of snakes, dragons, goats, etc., as symbols for the devil.

Satan can also appear as an "angel of light" in order to deceive people into thinking that he is an angel of God. In 2 Corinthians 11:14, the apostle Paul said this very thing. Is it any wonder then that he also sends out false prophets and false apostles who try to palm themselves off as God's servants? Appearances can be deceiving.

Christians must not be so gullible as to believe that if a being of light appears and talks sweetly to them that it automatically means the being is God, Jesus, or an angel from God. John tells us to test the spirits and gives guidelines for doing so:

> Beloved, do not believe every spirit, but test
> the spirits to see whether they are from God;
> because many false prophets have gone out

into the world. By this you know the Spirit
of God: every spirit that confesses that Jesus
Christ has come in the flesh is from God;
and every spirit that does not confess Jesus
is not from God; and this is the spirit of the
antichrist, of which you have heard that it
is coming, and now it is already in the world
(1 John 4:1-3).

It is in this sense that Paul warns us that if an
angel who claims to have come from heaven should
proclaim a different gospel, we must not believe him
(Galatians 1:8). If Joseph Smith would have followed
Paul's advice, the cult of Mormonism would have never
come into existence.

We need to warn people that Satan appears as a
beautiful angel of light (2 Corinthians 11:14). As the
father of all lies (John 8:44), he will claim to be God,
Jesus Christ, Mary, St. Jude, Muhammad, Krishna,
Shiva, Buddha, some alien from another planet, or whoever he needs to be in order to get people to worship and
obey him.

Remember, Satan does not appear and announce to
people that he is the devil and that he has come to damn
their souls. He claims the exact opposite.

Sometimes Satan and his demons pretend to be the
spirits of dead people. First Samuel 28:4-25 records a
time when Saul was in a difficult situation and tried
desperately to find out what he should do. God would not
answer his prayers because he was in sin. So Saul went
to a medium at Endor and asked her to call up his old
friend Samuel from the "world beyond" so he could get
some answers.

The medium held a seance for Saul. She was going
through her ritual, when all of a sudden, something
happened. The text indicates that this was not something she had planned. As is often the case, you often get
more than you expect in the occult.

The medium claimed that a form had appeared to her, and Saul assumed that the spirit of Samuel had indeed been brought back from the dead. But I don't believe it was Samuel. Many modern scholars agree it was actually a demon disguised as Samuel who appeared because:

1. Seances and mediumship are both condemned by God in Deuteronomy 18:9-11. In one of his better moments Saul had even made it illegal to engage in such activities (1 Samuel 28:9).

2. A medium does not have the power to call back the dead.

3. The medium referred to the manifestation as a "god" or "divine being" (verse 13). This can hardly refer to Samuel.

4. The medium was the only one who saw anything. Saul had to take her word for everything.

5. She described the "god" who appeared to her as being an old man wrapped in a robe (verse 14). This could have been anyone.

6. Saul fell on his face and worshiped this being (verse 14). It is highly doubtful that Samuel would have allowed himself to be worshiped as a god.

7. Saul wanted Samuel to tell him the future even though he admitted that God refused to tell him. But how could Samuel tell him about the future if God had already said no? Samuel could not know the future independently of God.

8. This "Samuel" predicted that Saul and his sons would be killed by the Philistines the very next day. But this did not happen the next day. In fact, Saul was not killed by the Philistines. He killed himself in an act of suicide (1 Samuel 31:4,5). It was thus a false prophecy.

9. Finally, people do not become ghosts when
   they die. Neither can they be contacted by
   mediums during seances.

A few scholars take the view that Samuel was actually brought back from the netherworld, but the text and its context seem to be clearly against this view.

•   •   •

As we have seen, Satan is a finite, created being who has delusions of grandeur in that he wants to be like the infinite God. He is very dangerous, but he can be defeated through the blood of the Lord Jesus Christ. Because of this, we are to fear God and not Satan.

3

Satan's Sure Defeat

As we stated in the last chapter, no Christian needs to live in the fear of Satan or his demons. The atoning work of Christ on the cross has secured the ultimate defeat of Satan. Thus the Christian is not fighting *for* victory but *from* victory.

Whether Satan or Christ wins in the end is not something yet to be decided by the roll of the dice. It is not something that is hanging in the balance. Christ's victory and Satan's downfall have already been infallibly secured.

The Mission of Christ

When Jesus Christ came to this earth, He immediately began to exercise His power upon Satan and his demons as He healed the sick, raised the dead, and cast out demons (Acts 10:38). Demons could not withstand His divine power.

When Jesus went to the cross for our sins, Satan rejoiced because he thought that he had defeated the Son of God. Little did he know that the cross would ultimately spell his doom. This is why the apostle Paul could boast in the cross of Christ (Galatians 6:14). The good news of the gospel is even called the "word of the cross" in 1 Corinthians 1:18 because it is by the cross that Satan has been defeated (Colossians 2:14,15).

The devil hates the cross of Christ because it is the glorious symbol of his defeat at the hands of the Son of God.

The Good News

The cross of Christ means that we are not fighting *for* victory but *from* victory. We fight *from* victory because of what Christ did on the cross (1 Corinthians 15:57). Jesus came into this world to save sinners (1 Timothy 1:15). But in order for Him to "save His people from their sins" (Matthew 1:21), He had to defeat the power and devices of Satan (Hebrews 2:14,15).

In Genesis 3:15, which is called the *proto-evangelicum*, the first preaching of the gospel, God said that He was going to send the "seed of the woman" and that the Seed would crush the head of the serpent. In other words, *someone* was going to come who would defeat the devices of Satan and undo all that the devil had done.

Hebrews 2:14-18 clearly states that Jesus Christ came that He might defeat Satan and thereby free the elect of God from the power the devil had over them.

The same thing is stated in 1 John 3:8, when it says that he who does what is sinful is of the devil because the devil has been sinning from the beginning (that is, from the very beginning of this world). The reason the Son of God came was to destroy the devil's works.

A Shackled Foe

We must realize that when Jesus Christ was on earth, He bound Satan.

When the Pharisees heard this, they said,
"It is only by Beelzebub, the prince of demons, that this fellow drives out demons."
Jesus knew their thoughts and said to them,
"Every kingdom divided against itself will
be ruined, and every city or household divided against itself will not stand. If Satan
drives out Satan, he is divided against himself. How then can his kingdom stand? And
if I drive out demons by Beelzebub, by whom
do your people drive them out? So then, they
will be your judges. But if I drive out demons
by the Spirit of God, then the kingdom of
God has come upon you. Or again, how can
anyone enter a strong man's house and
carry off his possessions unless he first ties
up the strong man? Then he can rob his
house" (Matthew 12:24-29 NIV).

In this passage the Lord Jesus Christ also denied
that He was a medium (something many New Age religions teach). He flatly rejected the idea that He was in
any way involved in cooperating with Satan. This is the
classic passage to use when dealing with those people
who believe that Jesus and Satan are walking down the
primrose path of life holding hands.

This passage also says that Jesus is robbing Satan's
kingdom of souls by driving out demons. This is what is
meant by Jesus' statement, "If I drive out demons."

In the Greek language there are four different
meanings for the English word *if*. One of these "ifs"
actually means "since" and assumes that what is pictured is a reality and not just a possibility.

Jesus uses this "if" in verse 28 when He says, "*If* I
drive out demons," meaning, "Since I do in fact drive out
demons."

There was no question of His driving out demons.
He began His public ministry by driving out a demon

(Mark 1:23-28). But how is it that Jesus delivered people who were possessed by demons? He attributes His power to two things:

First, He states in Matthew 12:28 that He drives out the demons "by the Spirit of God." Just as Jesus needed to be filled with the power of the Holy Spirit to defeat the demons, so do we.

One word of warning must be given at this juncture. Never attempt to deal with anyone who is possessed by demons unless you are filled with the power of the Holy Spirit. If you have unconfessed sin in your life, run the other way.

Second, Jesus clearly says in verse 29 that He is able to rob Satan of the souls held captive in his house because He has first bound him. How else can He steal sinners away from Satan's kingdom?

From the context of the passage, it is clear that Jesus was not talking about His second coming or the kingdom which He will establish on earth one day. We must not let our millennial expectations obscure the wonderful truth of the present binding of Satan. That Satan will be further bound in other ways in the future does not negate the fact that Jesus has bound him now.

It was His first coming that ushered in the present phase of His kingdom which we now call the church age. The words of Jesus cannot be avoided. Since He was driving out demons by the Spirit of God, then the kingdom of God had arrived in some form or the other.

Another passage which reveals the power of Jesus over the demons is John 12:31-33.

> "Now is the time for judgment on this world; now the prince of this world will be driven out. But I, when I am lifted up from the earth, will draw all men to myself." He said this to show the kind of death he was going to die (NIV).

The Lord Jesus Christ was saying that when He was lifted up on the cross, two things would happen. First, sinners from all races and ranks of humanity would be drawn to Him. And second, Satan would be judged. The judgment or the casting out of Satan actually began with the earthly ministry of the Lord Jesus Christ.

In John 16:11, we read, "In regard to judgment... the prince of this world now stands condemned" (NIV).

Because the present phase of the kingdom of God has been ushered in by the appearance of the King, because Jesus is now binding Satan and delivering sinners who are oppressed by the devil, because Satan's ultimate defeat was secured by the death of Christ on the cross, the sentence of condemnation has already been passed on Satan.

In Acts 10:38, the apostle Peter spoke of the power that Christ had over the demonic forces. He relates that God anointed Jesus of Nazareth with the Holy Spirit in power, and Jesus went about doing good and healing all who were "oppressed by the devil" because God was with Him.

The Gospels are filled with stories of the authority and the power that Christ had over the demons. They trembled in His presence and begged Him not to torment them.

When Jesus told the demons to leave the demoniac of the Gerasenes, they left (Mark 5:1-13). When He told them to enter the pigs, they entered the pigs. There was authority in His voice because Christ Jesus had come as the King of kings and the Lord of lords. The present phase of the kingdom of God had arrived upon earth. So we find the apostle Paul saying, "When He had disarmed the rulers and authorities, He made a public display of them, having triumphed over them through Him" (Colossians 2:15). By His atoning work on the cross, Jesus has secured the ultimate defeat of Satan.

Our Authority in Christ

The implications of Christ's victory over the devil are staggering. In Ephesians 2:6, Paul tells us that by virtue of our union with Christ, we are now seated in the heavenly places with Christ. With Him, we are now seated "above all rule and authority and power and dominion (Ephesians 1:21). Because of our union with Christ, we can be victorious over Satan! We have authority over the demons because of our position in Christ.

In Romans 16:20 the apostle Paul reminded the Romans of the prophecy found in Genesis 3:15 alluded to earlier, which referred to the seed of the woman who would trample Satan under His feet. Then he told the Christians at Rome that by virtue of their union with the seed of the woman, the Lord Jesus, "The God of peace will soon crush Satan under your feet." It is now not only the Lord Jesus who tramples the head of the serpent under His heel. The humblest child of God can trample Satan under his feet as well.

The Binding of Satan

In what sense is Satan "bound" today? Before the coming of Christ, Satan had universal sway over the nations of the earth, keeping them in the darkness of paganism and unbelief. This is why he could offer the kingdoms and power of this world to Christ when he tempted Him after His 40 days in the wilderness (Matthew 4:8,9). It is why he is called "the god of this world" (2 Corinthians 4:4).

Did the Babylonians worship the true God? No. Did the Phoenicians? No. Did the Incas? No. Did the Chinese? No. Did any of the great ancient civilizations worship the true God? No. They were all involved in idolatry (Romans 1:18-25) and the worship of demons (1 Corinthians 10:20). The end of these pagan nations is demonstrated in Psalm 9:17: "The wicked will return to Sheol, even all the nations who forget God."

Well, what about Israel? Much of the time they did not worship the living God either. They were always falling into idolatry and running after pagan religions. The sad story of how Israel constantly fell away from the truth into idolatry is recorded in the book of Judges.

Satan deceived the nations of this world and had them firmly in his grip. But notice what happened after Jesus came. Satan was now "bound" in the sense that he could no longer universally deceive the nations. The spell he had cast over the world was broken by the cross. Men and women from every tribe and tongue would now bow their knees to the one true God. Today people from every nation praise the Savior.

The universal sway of Satan over the nations has been bound during this present church age and will not be reestablished until the coming of the Antichrist and the false prophet. The door of the gospel is now open to all people everywhere. The "Great Commission" given in Matthew 28:19,20 contains the marching orders of King Jesus, who has all power and authority in heaven and on earth (Matthew 28:18).

4

A Classic Tale of Good and Evil

If Satan was originally created good, how, when, where, and why did he become evil?

Since the Bible was written for mankind and not for demons, it should not surprise us that it goes into more detail about the fall of man than it does the fall of Satan. Yet there are a few passages in the Scripture which deal with Satan's plummet into sin and guilt.

The Original Sin of Satan

In 1 Timothy 3:6 Paul tells us that the original sin of Satan was pride. In the context of this portion of Scripture, Paul is discussing the qualifications to be an elder. He says that an elder must not be a recent convert because he might become conceited and fall under the same judgment as the devil. We can conclude from this that the original sin of Satan was pride.

Pride is taking credit for things that only God can do or give. Pride is robbing God of the glory due to Him by trying to exalt or glorify yourself.

Humility is acknowledging that God is the One who made you different from other people and the One from whom you have received all that is good in your life (1 Corinthians 4:7). True humility is submitting to the sovereign will of God in order to glorify God instead of yourself.

Satan's Error

There are two classic passages in the Old Testament which have generally been applied to Satan. The first passage is Isaiah 14:4-21.

In his taunt of the king of Babylon, Isaiah suddenly stops attacking the king and addresses the evil one who was actually behind all the things that this king did:

> How you have fallen from heaven, O star of the morning, son of the dawn! You have been cut down to the earth, you who have weakened the nations! But you said in your heart, "I will ascend to heaven; I will raise my throne above the stars of God, and I will sit on the mount of assembly in the recesses of the north. I will ascend above the heights of the clouds; I will make myself like the Most High." Nevertheless you will be thrust down to Sheol, to the recesses of the pit (Isaiah 14:12-15).

Even though the immediate reference in this passage is to the king of Babylon, the ultimate reference would seem to be Satan. For example, since the king of Babylon was never in heaven, how could he fall down to the earth?

The second passage is Ezekiel 28:11-17:

> The word of the LORD came to me: "Son of man, take up a lament concerning the king of Tyre and say to him: 'This is what the

> sovereign LORD says, "You were the model of
> perfection, full of wisdom and perfect in
> beauty. You were in Eden, the garden of
> God; every precious stone adorned you; ruby,
> topaz and emerald, chrysolite, onyx and jas-
> per, sapphire, turquoise and beryl. Your
> settings and mountings were made of gold;
> on the day you were created they were pre-
> pared. You were anointed as a guardian
> cherub, for so I ordained you. You were on
> the holy mount of God; you walked among
> the fiery stones. You were blameless in your
> ways from the day you were created till
> wickedness was found in you. Through your
> widespread trade you were filled with vio-
> lence, and you sinned. So I drove you in
> disgrace from the mount of God, and I ex-
> pelled you, O guardian cherub, from among
> the fiery stones. Your heart became proud
> on account of your beauty, and you cor-
> rupted your wisdom because of your splen-
> dor. So I threw you to the earth"'" (NIV).

Once again, nothing in the passage could be literally applied to the king of Tyre. The king of Tyre was not
a model of perfection. Neither was he full of wisdom and
perfect in beauty. He wasn't in the Garden of Eden, nor
was he created sinless. He wasn't kicked out of heaven
and sent to the earth. So even though Ezekiel began his
lament against the earthly king of Tyre (verse 12), he
looked beyond the king to the evil one controlling him.

Combined with 1 Timothy 3:6, these two passages
are clear enough to indicate the original sin of Satan. He
desired to displace God, to be the center of glory and
honor and worship, and to be revered and feared. It was
through pride and conceit that he was lifted up and that
he was thrown down in judgment.

The Fall of Satan to Earth

Once Satan sinned, he was cast down to this planet. This "fall" is mentioned by Jesus in Luke 10:18: "I was watching Satan fall from heaven like lightning."

Wouldn't it have been wonderful if the devil had ended up on Mars instead of earth! We would have had a much happier time if he would have landed on some other planet. But once he was thrown down to this planet, he tempted Adam and Eve to join him in his rebellion against God (Genesis 3:1-6).

Not only does Satan roam the earth, it is also clear from the Scriptures that he still has limited access to heaven. According to Job 1:6, there was a time when the different angels were assembled before God. God saw Satan standing among them and said, in effect, "What are you doing here?"

Satan said, "I've been around patrolling the earth, taking a look at that planet."

Then God replied, "Well, did you happen to take notice of a man named Job?"

The devil said, "Oh yes, I know all about Job. You put a hedge around him, his family, and all his possessions. I can't touch him. That is the reason he worships You. If You take those things away from him, he will curse You to Your face."

God said, "You're wrong. Job loves Me for Me and not for the things I give him."

The devil laughed and said, "Take away all that stuff and he will curse You to Your face. Take away his possessions, take away his kids, take away his house, make his wife a curse to him, and he will curse You."

You know the rest of the story. The devil did his best to make Job curse God, but Job still worshiped and trusted the Lord.

The point is that evidently there are circumstances in which Satan is still allowed access to heaven. He can appear in the presence of God.

But what does he do there? Exactly what he did with Job. He accused Job of wrong motives in the worship of God. And today Satan remains the accuser of the brethren:

> Now have come the salvation and the power and the kingdom of our God, and the authority of his Christ. For the accuser of our brothers, who accuses them before our God day and night, has been hurled down (Revelation 12:10 NIV).

Satan still has limited access to heaven where he accuses us before God day and night. But we have an Advocate with the Father, Jesus Christ, who answers all of Satan's accusations on our behalf (1 John 2:1,2).

•   •   •

It was the sin of pride that turned the devil from good to evil. He wanted to glorify and exalt himself. Self-deification is the same sin which forms the basis of Eastern religions such as Hinduism and such Western movements as Mormonism and the New Age Movement. Anyone who claims that he is now divine or that he will become divine has fallen into a trap of Satan.

5

What's
in a Name?

What's in a name? In Scripture, names had a much greater significance than they do today. Most parents today do not choose a name for their children based on the meaning of the name. Instead, they choose a name that runs in the family or that is unique or popular.

In biblical times, names indicated something about the person who bore that name. They often indicated a character trait such as Jacob, which means "supplanter," or what a person did for a living. This held true for hundreds of years in Western culture and explains the origin of names such as Baker, Goldman, Taylor, Shepherd, etc. It is only in recent times that people's names have lost this sense of significance.

In this light, the biblical names and titles of this fallen angel who opposes all that is good and right indicate his nature and his work. Let us examine the names and titles of the devil in the order of their frequency of use in the Bible.

The Favorite Name
1. Satan. This fallen angel is called "Satan" 53

times in Scripture. It is the favorite name of the devil throughout the entire Bible. It is also his proper name. Thus when Jesus rebuked the devil when he had finished tempting Him, He used the devil's proper name. He said, "Begone, Satan!" (Matthew 4:10).

The word *Satan* in the Hebrew and Greek simply means "adversary." It refers to someone who is your enemy; someone who has it in for you. Remember those days in junior high when the school bully picked on you? Or maybe there was a girl who would gossip about you. You had an "adversary"—someone against you.

The Principle of First Mention

The first reference to "Satan" in the Bible is found in 1 Chronicles 21:1. As is often the case, the first mention of something or someone in the Bible is very important. It will therefore pay us to look more closely at this passage to see what it says about Satan:

> Then Satan stood up against Israel and moved David to number Israel (1 Chronicles 21:1).

The passage reveals several things:

Satan attacks nations as well as individuals. Both Israel and David came under attack. Satan's devices encompass a plan to destroy nations as well as the souls of men.

Satan has a special hatred for those nations where the truth is preached. We do not read that he "stood up against" nations that worshiped him through pagan religions. No. Instead, he lifted them up and sought to expand their power.

Satan is able to motivate people to do things by putting ideas in their minds. He put it into the mind of David to number the people. We'll have more to say about this later.

Satan can implant thoughts even in believers. David was not a pagan. Yet Satan was able to manipulate him into doing something that would harm both him and the nation.

Satan can take something which seems perfectly innocent and use it to do evil. Taking a census of men of fighting age is hardly wrong in and of itself. In the book of Numbers, God Himself commanded such a census be taken. Why then was it viewed as sin in this passage?

A clue is given in the response of Joab, the commander of David's armies. When David told Joab to number the people, Joab sensed that this was not the right thing to do at the time. There was no war. There was no need to enlarge the army. Besides, God had not commanded it. This is why Joab said, "May the LORD add to His people a hundred times as many as they are! But my lord the king, are they not all my lord's servants? Why does my lord seek this thing? Why should he be a cause of guilt to Israel?" (verse 3).

But when Satan is motivating someone to do something, it is very difficult to talk him out of it. So David did not listen to Joab and forced the census (verses 4,5).

Satan hates it when God's people love each other and are united in the cause of righteousness. The census caused a breach of fellowship between David and Joab, his best friend. Joab disobeyed David by not including the tribes of Levi and Benjamin in the census because he felt David's command was abhorrent (verse 6).

The census also caused fear, anger, and division among the people. Was the king going to attack a nation when there was no reason to do so? Was he out for vainglory like the pagan kings?

Satan wants to destroy a believer's walk with God and give God an occasion to punish him. Because David, Joab, and the nation of Israel fell into the sins of anger, strife, disunity, gossip, slander, etc., God had to condemn and punish them all (verse 7).

Satan loves it when personal sin leads others to wickedness. David confessed his sin in verse 8: "David said to God, 'I have sinned greatly, in that I have done this thing. But now, please take away the iniquity of Thy servant, for I have done very foolishly.'"

While God was merciful and forgave David his personal sin, this did not mean that everyone else was automatically forgiven.

God sent a plague and 70,000 people died under the wrath of God (verse 14)! The city of Jerusalem was almost destroyed (verse 15). Satan laughed as he saw the damage he had done to Israel, David, and Joab.

Just from this brief look at the text we see that from the very first mention, the being named "Satan" is the enemy of all that is good. He actively seeks to destroy the unity of God's people on an individual and corporate level.

Other Old Testament Mentions

Not only is Satan mentioned in the historical section of the Old Testament, he is also mentioned in the poetical sections.

In the oldest book of the Bible, the book of Job, the name "Satan" pops up in the very first chapter. The oldest name in the oldest book for the evil one is "Satan"!

Once again, Satan is the "adversary" of the people of God, which is why he sought to destroy Job and his family. Satan's insanity is obvious to all who read how he desperately tried to get Job to curse God.

When we turn to the section of the Old Testament referred to as the Prophets, we are once again confronted with this insane being who was cast down to this planet and who is determined to destroy the people of God:

> Then he showed me Joshua the high priest standing before the angel of the LORD, and

Satan standing at his right side to accuse
him. And the LORD said to Satan, "The LORD
rebuke you, Satan! Indeed, the LORD who
has chosen Jerusalem rebuke you! Is this
not a brand plucked from the fire?" (Zechariah 3:1,2).

While Joshua the high priest was interceding for
Israel, Satan was standing at his right hand as his
adversary. The LORD had to rebuke Satan in order for
Joshua to get on with the holy task of interceding for the
people of God.

Satan in the New Testament

The name "Satan" is also found in the Gospels,
where it is the predominant name for this fallen angel.
In Matthew 4:10 it was "Satan" who came and tempted
the Lord Jesus. He had the nerve to try and tempt even
the Lord Jesus!

The apostle Peter was familiar with Satan on a
firsthand basis. No doubt he painfully remembered the
time that Satan put the idea into his mind to rebuke the
Lord Jesus (Matthew 16:22). I know that I would never
forget that awful incident if it had happened to me.

When Peter opened his mouth and rebuked the Son
of God, Jesus turned around and in front of everyone
rebuked Satan for putting Peter up to it (Matthew
16:23). I would not have wanted to be in Peter's shoes on
that day!

In Acts 26:17,18 the apostle Paul speaks of the
commission that the Lord Jesus Christ gave to him at
his conversion:

I will rescue you from your own people and
from the Gentiles. I am sending you [Paul]
to them to open their eyes and turn them

from darkness to light, and from the power
of Satan to God, so that they may receive
forgiveness of sins and a place among those
who are sanctified by faith in me (NIV).

At the very inception of Paul's Christian experience, Jesus sent him forth to preach a message which
would open spiritual eyes and turn sinners from darkness to light. Paul would see the gospel release people
from the powerful grasp of Satan and transfer them into
the kingdom of Christ (Colossians 1:13).

In Paul's letters to the church at Rome, Christians
are told to rejoice because they will crush Satan under
their feet (Romans 16:20). In the New Testament letters
known as the General Epistles, Satan is the predominant name for the devil. In Revelation, the final judgment and doom of Satan is revealed. He and his fellow
fallen angels "will be tormented day and night" (Revelation 20:10).

The Bible talks about the future as something that
is certain because God has ordained it to come to pass.
As surely as you are reading this book right now, the
doom of Satan has already been set in motion. It is what
is called in the business world "a done deal."

Scripture describes the future with the same certainty with which it describes the past. God will triumph
over the devil. The good will win over the evil. Justice
shall be vindicated. Christ will judge the world in righteousness, and the saints will live happily forever. The
future is not a cosmic crap game ruled by Lady Luck.
Since God is the sovereign Creator and Sustainer of the
universe, He will bring His words to pass (1 Thessalonians 5:24).

His Most-Used Title

2. Devil. The most-used *title* (as opposed to *Satan*,
which is the most-used name) in Scripture for Satan is

the New Testament word *devil.* It is a Greek word which literally means "tempter." It is a title instead of a name because it is not a proper name at all. This is why it is not capitalized in the Bible.

Satan is called the "devil" 31 times in the New Testament because he tempts people to do evil. Biblical authors will often use the word *devil* instead of some other title when temptation is the specific device of Satan under consideration.

As Jesus began His public ministry, He was led by the Spirit to spend 40 days in the wilderness. We saw earlier that during this time Jesus was visited by Satan. Since the purpose of Satan's visit was to tempt Jesus, Matthew and Luke both use the title "devil" in their accounts of the temptation (Matthew 4:1-11; Luke 4:1-13).

In his description of the temptation, Matthew uses the title "devil" four times (Matthew 4:1,5,8,11) and the title "tempter" once (Matthew 4:3). The use of the word *tempter* in verse 3 emphasized the particular device Satan employed.

Matthew introduces the name "Satan" only when he quotes Jesus' rebuke of the devil in Matthew 4:10. "Satan" refers to the person while "devil" refers to the work. You could say that "*Satan* is the name while the word *devil* is the game." Hence the name "Satan" was used when Jesus officially rebuked him and ordered him to leave.

In Acts 10:38, we read how "God anointed Jesus of Nazareth with the Holy Spirit and power, and how he went around doing good and healing all who were under the power of the devil, because God was with him" (NIV).

Notice that Peter summarized the earthly ministry of Jesus in terms of His power to deliver people from the power of the devil.

Paul also used the word *devil* when he rebuked a witch. His scathing rebuke serves as a model of how to answer modern occultists and heretics:

> Then Saul, who was called Paul, filled with
> the Holy Spirit, looked straight at Elymas
> and said, "You are a child of the devil and an
> enemy of everything that is right! You are
> full of all kinds of deceit and trickery. Will
> you never stop perverting the right ways of
> the Lord?" (Acts 13:9,10 NIV).

Paul's rebuke would no doubt be condemned as
"unloving" by those who think that someone's feelings
are more important than God's truth or their immortal
soul. But notice that it was the Spirit of God who led
Paul to rebuke this witch as a "child of the devil."

Career Soldiers

In Ephesians 6:11,12, the apostle Paul describes
the Christian life as a battle with the devil:

> Put on the full armor of God so that you can
> take your stand against the devil's schemes.
> For our struggle is not against flesh and
> blood, but against the rulers, against the
> authorities, against the powers of this dark
> world and against the spiritual forces of evil
> in the heavenly realms (NIV).

The Christian life is a spiritual war in which the
believer is a soldier who needs his full armor to defeat
the temptations of the devil.

Peter was tempted by the devil to rebuke the Lord
and then tempted yet again to deny the Lord. It is no
wonder that he described the devil as a vicious lion. He
had been mauled by that old wicked lion and warned us
from his own experience:

> Be self-controlled and alert. Your enemy
> the devil prowls around like a roaring lion

looking for someone to devour. Resist him,
standing firm in the faith, because you
know that your brothers throughout the
world are undergoing the same kind of sufferings (1 Peter 5:8,9 NIV).

Please notice that the "roaring lion" is after Christians, not unbelievers. I have been mauled a few times
myself and expect to feel the devil's teeth now and then
as I rob him of souls in the future. There is a price to pay
when you fight the devil.

Other Names and Titles

3. Dragon. The next most-used title for Satan was
a popular intertestamental Jewish literary description.
Since the book of Revelation was written in the style of a
Jewish apocalyptic work, it is no surprise to find that it
calls Satan a "dragon" 13 times. In Revelation 12:9 the
dragon is identified as Satan, the devil, and the serpent
all rolled into one evil being.

The Jews used the dragon as a symbol of the devil
because it was traditionally viewed as loathsome, evil,
vile, and malicious. This is in keeping with the picture of
the dragon in Revelation as one who seeks to devour the
saints (see also Revelation 12–13).

4. The Evil One. The devil is called "the evil one"
12 times in the Bible. How appropriate! For that is
exactly what he is by nature. With this title we enter the
realm of his character.

Most people do not realize that where our English
translation of the "Lord's Prayer" says, "Deliver us from
evil," the Greek actually says, "Deliver us from the evil
one," in other words, the devil! Even in His high-priestly
prayer in John 17, Jesus said, "I do not ask Thee to take
them out of the world, but to keep them from the evil
one" (John 17:15).

Not only do we find the devil described as the "evil one" in the Gospels, but we later find that the apostle John rejoiced because the young men had "overcome the evil one" (1 John 2:13). Then in 1 John 5:18, we read one of the most precious promises in all the Bible. The apostle of love tells us that ultimately the evil one cannot harm the child of God. Satan may scratch and maul you, but he cannot really harm you. Even old Job was better off in the end than at the beginning.

5. Baalzebub or Beelzebub. The devil is called "Baalzebub" or "Beelzebub" 11 times in the Bible. The Hebrew word literally means "Lord of the Flies" and originally referred to the Egyptian worship of the sun god called "Baal" as "the lord of the flies." The Egyptians even worshiped the fly itself. Archaeologists have dug up idols in the form of the common housefly.

It became a Jewish name for Satan and is referred to in the Old Testament in 2 Kings 1:2,3,6,16 and is used in the Gospels seven times. As a matter of fact, it was one of Jesus' favorite terms.

6. The Serpent. Satan is called a serpent or a snake ten times in the Bible. The first reference to Satan as a snake is found in Genesis 3, where Satan spoke through the body of a snake.

In the New Testament, a serpent is referred to in 2 Corinthians 11:3, where the apostle Paul worried that just as that old "snake" deceived Eve, he was going to deceive them. Again in Revelation 12:9 and 20:2 the devil is called that "serpent of old," a reference to the fact that he was with man and woman in the garden.

It is interesting to note that occultists and New Agers have turned dragons and snakes into symbols of goodness and even wear them as good luck charms. But all this recent glorification of dragons and snakes is just another attempt by Satan to get people to worship him. We should educate our children that such things are symbols of *evil*.

7. The Prince of this Age. The apostle John called the devil "the prince of this age" (NIV) three times (John 12:31; 14:30; 16:11). The King James translates it as "the prince of this world," but the Greek word that is translated "world" does not refer to this planet but rather to an age. Thus he is called "the prince of this age" in modern translations.

Satan has only this age in which to fight against God and His people. His days are numbered, and he knows it.

8. The Adversary. Satan is called "the Adversary" (or "enemy") twice in the New Testament (1 Timothy 5:14 and 1 Peter 5:8). He is the adversary of the souls of men and opposes all that is righteous.

9. The Prince of Demons. The devil is called "the prince of demons" two times (Matthew 9:34 and 12:24 NIV). That he is called the "prince" or "ruler" of the demons indicates that the demons are not a disorganized mob. There is a chain of command, and Satan is the boss. Demons are under his authority.

10. The Prince of the Power of the Air. Satan is called "the prince of the power of the air" in Ephesians 2:2 because his kingdom is universal and invisible just like air. When asked where Satan rules, the rabbis would wave their hands in the air to symbolize that his invisible rule was everywhere.

11. The God of this Age. Satan is called "the god of this age" in 2 Corinthians 4:4 (NIV) because his goal is to keep people in this age from hearing and believing the glorious gospel by blinding their minds to the truth.

The word *god* here is used in the figurative sense, in the same way pagan idols are called "gods." They are not "gods" by nature but only by name (Galatians 4:8).

12. The Accuser of the Brethren. The title "the accuser of [the] brethren" is used in Revelation 12:10 as a title for Satan. When I meet Christians whose "ministry" is to run around and accuse the brethren all the time, I assume that they are on the devil's payroll because they are doing his work for him!

God has called all Christians to defend the faith according to Jude 3. Our focus should be on defending the gospel when unbelievers attack it and not on attacking the character and motives of fellow Christians (1 Corinthians 4:1-5).

When Peter tells us in 1 Peter 3:15 to give a logical answer to those people who challenge the gospel, he goes on to say that we should be gentle and respectful as we do this. Remember, it is not enough to win the argument. Our goal is to win the person to Christ!

13. The Spirit of Disobedience. In Ephesians 2:2 the devil is called "the spirit who is now at work in those who are disobedient" (NIV) because he is a malignant fiend who loves to motivate people to rebellion and anarchy.

Having pastored for many years, I have seen far too many people fall into this device of Satan by becoming disobedient and rebellious to the rule of Christ over His church. My heart has been broken so many times by people who rebel against the lordship of Christ by demanding their own way in church affairs.

Like the man mentioned in 3 John 9, they are determined to either rule or ruin the local church they attend. In some cases, they split one church after another out of rebellion to the rule of Christ and then have the gall to claim they have done God a favor. Their condemnation is just.

No wonder the apostle Paul came down hard on the demonic spirit of disobedience that caused so much pain and suffering in the churches he founded. In this rebellious age we must learn to submit to the lordship of Christ in all of life and follow what He has set forth in His Word concerning the structure, offices, and management of the local church (1 Thessalonians 5:12,13; Hebrews 13:17).

14. The Deceiver of the Whole World. This title is given to the devil in Revelation 12:9, and who can argue with it?

15. Abaddon or Apollyon. Satan is called in the Hebrew, *Abaddon*, and in the Greek, *Apollyon*, in Revelation 9:11. Both words simply mean the "destroyer," one who loves to mangle, to rip, or to tear. Don't think for one minute that those whose main "ministry" is destroying the lives and families of God's people are ministers of God.

16. The Father of Lies. Satan is called the "father of lies" by Jesus in John 8:44. Do you want to know the origin of all lies? The lie that we are all a part of God? The lie that we oozed out of God and are oozing back into God? They came from the "father of lies."

One new device of Satan that has recently gained popularity is the idea that it is not "loving" to tell people the truth. Anything that might hurt someone's feelings is viewed as unloving. This lie pits love against truth. We should never allow this to happen.

The apostle Paul admonished Christians to speak "the truth in love" (Ephesians 4:15). There is no conflict between speaking the truth and loving someone. The conflict is between coddling someone's feelings and loving them enough to tell them the truth.

17. The King over the Demons. The devil is called the king over the demons in Revelation 9:11 because he is their leader and they are his followers.

18. The Tempter. As we noted earlier, Satan is called "the tempter" in Matthew 4:3 and 1 Thessalonians 3:5. Paul says to the Thessalonians:

> For this reason, when I could stand it no longer, I sent to find out about your faith. I was afraid that in some way the tempter might have tempted you and our efforts might have been useless (NIV).

19. Lucifer. Satan may or may not be called "Lucifer" in Isaiah 14:12. Most Hebrew scholars feel that "Lucifer" is not the proper translation of the Hebrew word—that the Hebrew actually refers to him as the "shining one," he who had the brightness of God's glory originally shining around him. That is why most modern translations do not use the name "Lucifer" in the text.

20. Archangel. Down through the centuries, it has been speculated that Satan was an archangel because he is compared to the archangel Michael in Jude 9 and in Revelation 12:7-12.

The Bible uses the word *archangel* only in reference to Michael. We do not have a single verse where Satan is specifically called an archangel. But while the word *archangel* is not used of Satan, he and Michael are linked together in several passages in a way that seems to put them on equal footing. This is why many Christians have assumed that Satan was originally an archangel.

It would also seem that Satan may be more powerful than Michael because Michael could not personally rebuke him:

> But even the archangel Michael, when he was disputing with the devil about the body of Moses, did not dare to bring a slanderous accusation against him [Satan], but said "The Lord rebuke you!" (Jude 9 NIV).

If Michael were equal to or greater than the devil, he could have rebuked Satan.

•   •   •

With all these names and titles, it is obvious that the Bible means to indicate that Satan is an evil *being* and not just a *symbol* of evil. He is a fallen angel of vast power and intellect who migrated to this planet along with his evil followers. And he insanely imagines that he can become God.

Satan's insanity has led him to oppose all that is good and right and to oppose all life and love. But his ultimate defeat at the hands of Jesus has been secured by Christ's death on the cross. The victory belongs to Jesus!

6

What Satan Can and Cannot Do

Now that we understand more about Satan's nature, we can look more directly at his powers and abilities. What can Satan do and what can he not do according to the Bible?

In this chapter we are going to overview Satan's *present* powers. We are not talking about what he was like in heaven before he fell, or what he could do in the Garden of Eden, or what he could do while Christ was on earth. We are talking about *now*—the present age.

We want to look at his present abilities because this is where we live, and it's important to know what he is like and what he can do today.

Once again we have to avoid the two great dangers of 1) attributing far too much power to Satan and living in fear of him or 2) attributing far too little power to Satan and failing to view him as a real threat. There is much confusion and false teaching about the devil, so we must be very careful not to take extreme positions but to search for a biblical balance.

Why do some people not view Satan and his demons as threats? The reasons are many and varied, but primarily such people assume that the devil and his demons have to do with an era long past and have nothing to do with the present. Satan belongs to biblical times and the age of miracles. There is no danger today that someone could be demon possessed or that satanic miracles could happen. All that devil stuff is over. It does not happen in the modern world.

The reason that some pastors and theologians deny the existence of satanic miracles today is that they also deny that God does any miracles today. They first limit what God can do and then go on to limit what the devil can do.

I readily admit that if God cannot do any miracles today, and Satan can still do miracles, we are all in big trouble. Since these same people deny that we can have the power of the Holy Spirit today, then logically they must also deny that the power of Satan is still operative or we would be left utterly defenseless against him.

The Apostolic Age

Those who deny that Satan can do miracles today begin with the assumption that church history can be divided into two watertight periods, the "apostolic age" and the "church age."

According to this view, the apostolic age began with John the Baptist and ended with the death of the last apostle (or the death of the last person upon whom the last apostle had literally laid his hands in blessing).

This apostolic age was the age of miracles—divine and satanic. But when this age ended, all miracles ceased. Miracles were given for only one purpose: to validate the apostles' credentials. Once the apostles' authority had been validated, we did not need miracles anymore. Once the Bible was finished, there was no longer any reason for miracles.

Those people who hold to this belief are in a difficult position. If you tell them of miracles that you have seen or experienced yourself, the incidents must be dismissed as frauds, mental illness, or psychosomatic healings.

If you tell them of demon possession, it must be set aside as some kind of psychological problem.

If you relate the many "miracles" found in the cults and the occult, they will tell you that all psychic events and experiments are frauds. Psychics and channelers are all phonies. Nobody levitates anything. Nobody apports anything. There is no reality whatsoever to psychic phenomena. All is fraud and trickery.

But is it? Is there any Scripture in the Old or New Testaments which speaks of a special "apostolic age"? There are verses that talk about the Old Covenant and verses that talk about the New Covenant, but nowhere in the Bible does it refer to an "apostolic age" within the New Covenant. Do any Scriptures state clearly that when the last apostle died, all miracles ceased? Also, does church history show a clear cutoff point for all divine and satanic miracles? That is, were there still demon-possessed people and healings after the last apostle died? Did the early church understand that all miracles ceased in the "apostolic age"? And finally, where in the Bible does it tell us that Satan cannot do miracles today?

There is no Scripture to support the idea that all divine and satanic miracles ceased the day the last apostle died. On the other hand, there are dozens of New Testament passages that tell us that Satan is alive and doing well on planet Earth. He has not retired from his nefarious schemes. He is not quietly sitting in a wheelchair somewhere awaiting his day of judgment. He still thinks that he will win in the end.

Peter had learned the hard way about the present power of the evil one. This is why he warned us in 1 Peter 5:8,9:

> Be of sober spirit, be on the alert. Your
> adversary, the devil, prowls about like a
> roaring lion, seeking someone to devour.
> But resist him, firm in your faith, knowing
> that the same experiences of suffering are
> being accomplished by your brethren who
> are in the world.

It is clear that Peter was addressing Christians and
that he was warning them that the devil was their
enemy. There is no indication in the text that this was
true only for his day and that the devil would no longer
roar in our day.

Neither is there anything in Ephesians 6:10-20 to
indicate that spiritual warfare against the powers of
darkness was something just for the apostles until the
last of them died. As a matter of fact, if we were to go
through the New Testament with a pair of scissors and
cut out all the references to Satan and say, "Well, these
verses were just for the apostolic age," we would destroy
much of the New Testament.

What Can Satan Do?

If we can agree that Satan is still actively opposing
God and those who are saved by God, then the question
naturally arises, what can Satan and his demons do?

First, keep in mind that demons are all fallen
angels, and thus they are far superior to man in strength,
intelligence, and abilities.

Please notice that Satan and the demons are able to
do what is natural for all angels to do. For example, just
as a good angel can materialize into human form, so can
the devil and his demons. In this sense, the powers of
Satan and his demons are natural angelic powers and do
not arise from their fall into sin.

Teleportation

Demons, like all angels, are capable of teleportation. In other words, they can travel through space from one place to another in an instant. For example, they can go from Europe to Africa a lot faster than the Concord. This is why medieval artists pictured angels as having wings. They travel swiftly through the air from one place to another as if they had wings.

But even greater is their ability to travel through different dimensions. For example, in Job 1:6,7, Satan "popped" into heaven and then he "popped" right back to earth to irritate poor Job. Thus demons can move dimensionally as well as spatially.

Visible Manifestations

A demon can manifest or produce visible, physical materializations in various forms. It can appear as a man, a woman, a snake, a dog, a goat, or even as an angel of light (2 Corinthians 11:14). They can appear as anything they want. During seances and various magic rituals, manifestations are sometimes seen coming out of the demon-possessed medium. They are quite real and can be touched.

Good angels as well as bad angels evidently have the ability to materialize in human forms. Remember the two good-looking "men" who walked into Sodom and created a riot among the homosexuals (Genesis 19)? Or the two young "men" who sat by the open tomb and announced the resurrection of Christ (Luke 24:4)? Or the two "men" who announced that Jesus would return one day (Acts 1:10,11)? These "men" were all angels who temporarily made themselves visible in human form.

Apportation

Demons can "apport" objects. In other words, they can move things and people from place to place through supernatural means. The word *apport* simply means to take an object and make it disappear in one place and reappear in another place.

One clear example can be found in Matthew 4:5,8, where Satan took Jesus and moved Him from the desert to the pinnacle of the temple and then moved Him from the temple to the top of a high mountain.

Levitation

One form of apportation is levitation, in which an object or person defies gravity, rises up, and floats in the air through supernatural means.

The devil evidently has the ability to levitate. In Matthew 4, just as Satan moved Jesus from one place to another, he also levitated Him up from the ground to the top of the temple.

Since demons can "fly" through the air, they are capable of defying gravity. It is no wonder that they can at times lift up people and things and make them float around the room as well. This is the origin of all the stories of "flying" witches and "floating" gurus who moved from one place to another through the air.

Visions

In Matthew 4:8, Satan "showed" Jesus all the kingdoms of this world with all their glory. How did he do this? One possible way he could have done this was to create a three-dimensional picture in the air which showed the glory of the nations passing in review.

This is the kind of thing that Satan does in the occult. Witches and magicians see many strange things while engaged in occultic rituals. We know of one instance in which an occultist was given a "holographic" vision of the throne and majesty of Satan and was so overwhelmed by what he saw that he thought it the throne of God!

It should not surprise us that Satan tries to imitate God by giving visions. God has been giving visions to His prophets since the beginning of time. What do you think happened to Peter in Joppa when he "fell into a trance" on the roof (Acts 10:10-16)? He "saw" a sheet lowered down out of heaven three times and a herd of animals ran out of the sheet each time. Then the sheet was taken back up into heaven. In other words, Peter saw a three-dimensional full-color picture floating in thin air.

Predictions of the Future

Throughout history, God has told His servants what is going to happen in the future. These predictions are always 100 percent accurate, certain, and infallible. Only God knows what will happen in the future because He has sovereignly decreed all that will come to pass. For example, everything that was prophesied in the Old Testament about Christ's first coming was fulfilled in the New Testament.

As we've noted, Satan always tries to copy God, and it stands to reason that he would delude people with false predictions. The only problem is that he cannot pull this off in the end because he is *not* God. He is only an angel with delusions of grandeur who likes to think of himself as a god.

The false prophets in the Old Testament and the fortune-tellers mentioned in the New Testament are examples of Satan's delusion, "If God can do it, so can I." But this claim is pure nonsense. Satan cannot know or control the future. He himself is part of the eternal plan of God (Proverbs 16:4).

The devil does not have any of God's infinite attributes, including omniscience. He does not and cannot know what is going to happen in the future. But this does not stop him from pretending that he knows it.

Indeed, predicting the future via astrology, palm reading, Ouija boards, crystal balls, etc., is the main money-maker in the occult. Billions of dollars are wasted each year by people who ask occultists to tell them the future.

If the devil knew the future, his servants would be able to make 100 percent accurate predictions—yet they cannot.

Matter Transformation

The transformation of matter is the actual or seeming changing of matter from one molecular form into another. Jesus did this when He changed the water into wine (John 2:1-11). Moses did this when he changed water into blood (Exodus 7:15-20). Aaron also did this when he threw down his staff, and it became a snake (Exodus 7:9,10).

The reason that Pharaoh was not that impressed was that he had court magicians who could do what Aaron and Moses had done. They turned water into blood and threw down their sticks and they became snakes as well (Exodus 7:11,22). Satan was trying to match God miracle by miracle.

The only way for Aaron to show that his miracle was of God was to have his snake eat the other snakes (Exodus 7:12). That was some feat! But it still did not impress Pharaoh.

Counterfeit Miracles

Satan loves to duplicate the miracles that God does even if he has to cheat to do it. This is why he is said to do "counterfeit miracles, signs and wonders" in 2 Thessalonians 2:9 (NIV).

The word *counterfeit* reveals that since Satan and his demons are not really capable of doing every kind of miracle that God does, they will use some kind of trick, fraud, or illusion to make it appear that they can.

These "counterfeit" miracles may at times be so clever and deceptive that no one can discover how the fraud is done. But it is a fraud nonetheless. The key is to remember that when we are confronted with what looks like a real miracle done by a pagan, cultist, occultist, or New Ager, we must begin with the assumption that it is a "counterfeit" miracle until we have the opportunity to check it out.

Spontaneous Combustion

"Spontaneous combustion" refers to those instances where animals or people are literally burned up by some kind of supernatural agency.

On different occasions God has literally burned up individuals and even groups of people. The "fire" which consumed Ahaziah's men when they were in the open may have been lightning (2 Kings 1:9-12). But when the fire came out from the altar and consumed people, some means other than lightning was being used (see Leviticus 9:24; 10:2; Numbers 11:1-3; 26:10).

Evidently, Satan also has the ability to materialize fire out of nowhere and burn people and things up. In Job 1:16, Satan sent down fire and consumed both animals and men. It may have been lightning. We are not told what it was beyond the fact that it was a satanic miracle.

In Revelation 13:13, one of the ways that the Antichrist will amaze people is by being able to cause "fire" to materialize out of thin air in the presence of men. In the context, this "fire" will probably be used to consume his enemies just like God's fire did to Ahaziah's men.

Demon Possession

Satan and his demons can possess the minds of non-Christians. Paul says in 2 Timothy 2:26 that Satan can take an unbeliever at will! This is what he did to Judas according to John 13:27. In the New Testament, demon possession is viewed as being different from physical and mental illness (Mark 1:32-34). It is not just a trick or con game. This is such an important subject that we will devote an entire chapter to it later on in this book.

Plant Thoughts

Satan can "read" our minds and even put ideas into our minds. Who put it into the mind of David to count the people of Israel? According to 1 Chronicles 21:1, it was Satan. Who put it into the mind of Peter that Jesus should not die? According to Matthew 16:22,23, it was Satan.

The implantation of thoughts is a very vigorous form of telepathy and is never a one-way street. Instead of just reading our thoughts, demons can also project a thought into our minds.

The Power to Kill

Satan evidently has the ability to kill disobedient Christians as well as non-Christians. This is what he did to the children and servants of Job (Job 1:13-19). When a professing Christian is delivered unto Satan "for the destruction of his flesh," Satan is allowed to kill that person (1 Corinthians 5:5).

Hinder Understanding

Satan can hinder man's ability to comprehend the gospel:

> And even if our gospel is veiled, it is veiled
> to those who are perishing, in whose case

> the god of this world has blinded the minds
> of the unbelieving, that they might not see
> the light of the gospel of the glory of Christ,
> who is the image of God (2 Corinthians
> 4:3,4).

This explains the spiritual blindness we see around us today.

Bodily Illnesses

Satan can inflict people with bodily illness, but not all bodily illness is demonic. For example, in the healings of Jesus, sometimes illness was demon produced (Matthew 8:16; Mark 1:32-34; 9:17), but other times it was not.

If people were blind, deaf, and mute because of the presence of a demon, the person would be able to hear, see, and speak when the demon was removed. But that does not mean that all bodily illness is demon-related.

Mental Illness

Satan can inflict mental illness. In Mark 5:1-15, the man who lived among the tombs and broke every chain that was placed on him was suicidal, homicidal, and had tremendous mental problems. Yet after Jesus commanded the evil spirit to come out of him, the man regained his right mind.

Incite Opposition to God

Satan incites opposition to God. When Paul set out on his missionary journey in Acts 13:6-12, there was opposition from a demon-possessed magician. The occult has always been the enemy of God.

Remove the Word of God

Satan can remove the Word of God from the mind of a person who doesn't understand it (Matthew 13:19). How he does this is not given in the text. But we can assume that he primarily removes the Word by distracting the mind with other things so that the person does not give heed to what he has heard (Hebrews 4:1,2).

Weather Manipulation

Both God and Satan can manipulate the weather (Exodus 9:22-25; Mark 4:35-39). In Mark 4:37, I believe with many commentators that Satan sent a violent storm to kill Jesus while He was asleep on the boat. It was rebuked because Satan was trying to kill Him. Satan also caused a great wind to come and knock down the house and kill Job's children (Job 1:18,19).

Hinder Answers to Prayer

According to Daniel 10:12-14,20,21, Satan and his cronies hindered Daniel from receiving an answer to his prayers. In this passage, it seems that the "hindering" had to do with keeping an angel of God from reaching Daniel for 21 days. This angel was evidently stopped by a demon who was too strong for him. So he had to get Michael to break through the blockade.

Since this is the *only* passage in the Bible which pictures the demons hindering answers to prayer, we are left with all sorts of questions for which there are no answers. We will have to content ourselves with the text as it is given and not speculate any further.

This passage reveals that some angelic beings are stronger than others. The same idea is also implied in the New Testament, where the demonic host is broken down into the categories of rule, authority, power, and dominion in such places as Ephesians 1:21.

This should not come as a surprise. Satan is the most powerful of the fallen angels and sits as their king. His followers are no doubt arranged in some kind of rank and file in the same way that human governments and armies are structured.

Tempt to Evil

Satan is called the "tempter" because he actively solicits and incites angels and men to rebel against God (1 Thessalonians 3:5).

False Religions

Satan invents all false religions and heretical ideas (2 Corinthians 11:3,4; 1 Timothy 4:1-3; 1 John 4:1-3). He is the father of all lies according to Jesus in John 8:44.

Control Animals

Aaron was able to call forth billions of frogs to torment the people of Egypt (Exodus 8:5,6). But the magicians of Pharaoh did the same with their occultic powers (Exodus 8:7).

In the New Testament, even pigs came under control of demons (Mark 5:12,13). Thus animals can be used by demons just as they can be used by the Lord. Remember the poor snake that Satan used to speak to Eve or the birds that God used to feed Elijah? Animals can be used either way.

Healings

Demons can produce "counterfeit" healings in the sense that whatever disease the demons give to a person, they can take back when they desire. Thus they can afflict someone with sickness and then remove it in order to counterfeit a healing. We find multiple examples of this in the occult and in the cults such as Christian Science.

Speaking in Tongues

There are many types of "speaking in tongues." There is divine speaking in tongues, a psychological speaking in tongues, and a satanic speaking in tongues. The early Mormons spoke in tongues just as the Aryan cult called The Way International teaches their disciples to speak in tongues. Many occultic groups practice speaking in tongues.

Financial Affairs

Satan can manipulate things to bring people financial disaster or wealth. He can make you rich or he can make you poor. Didn't he do this to Job? He took the richest man on the face of the earth and turned him into a pauper.

Can he make people rich? He tried this approach with Jesus. Satan showed Jesus all the glory and the riches of the world that he would give Him if only Jesus would fall down and worship him.

It is interesting to note that many of the great occultists died in poverty and loneliness. Whereas Jesus usually saves the best for last (John 2:10), the devil gives the worst in the end.

Inciting Disunity

Satan can disrupt the assembly of the saints by his presence or by inciting disunity, lies, gossip, slander, and divisions (Acts 5 and 6; 1 and 2 Corinthians).

Depression

Satan can keep believers in a constant state of

depression and discouragement if we do not resist him so that he will flee from us. That is why Peter warned believers in 1 Peter 5:8,9 about the devil's desire to devour us.

Buffeting Believers

Satan can "buffet" a believer (2 Corinthians 12:7). What was this "messenger of Satan"? We are not told. Most scholars believe that Paul was referring to poor eyesight. But whatever it was, it was used of God to keep Paul humble.

The Occult

Satan can communicate with people during seances and other occultic rites. He can give information which is supernatural in origin. He can tell them things which no one could know by any other means than a divine or supernatural source.

This is how some occultists can come up with your name and Social Security number. He or she either got the information naturally by some trick or supernaturally from a demon.

Sexual Encounters

We already established that angels can materialize a human body. It is therefore not surprising to find many examples in history where demons supposedly "put on" a male or female body and then engaged in sex with humans. This may sound farfetched, but let me point out several passages in the Bible which might also point in this direction, along with a number of interpretations people have given them.

First, in the oldest book in the Bible, Job, angels

are called "the sons of God" in 1:6, 2:1, and 38:7. That this title was later used to refer to believers is unrelated to the issue of its original meaning.

The early tradition of calling angels "the sons of God" was carried into the time of the kings (Psalm 29:1 and 89:7 in the Hebrew text) and the prophets (Daniel 3:25). It was used throughout the Old Testament as a title for angels.

Genesis 6:2 mentions "sons of God" who had sex with human females and produced the "giants," called Nephilim. Moses did not explain to his readers what the phrase "the sons of God" meant, which strongly implies that he assumed his readers already knew.

Since Job was the only biblical book in existence before Moses wrote Genesis, the only possible literary reference to "the sons of God" would be to angels. Thus the angelic interpretation is hermeneutically the assumption with which we should begin.

When this is combined with the fact that the phrase was not used by Moses in Genesis to describe the descendants of Seth, it presents a strong case in favor of the angelic interpretation.

The ancient Jews believed that the phrase "the sons of God" referred to fallen angels who had sex with human females and produced a bastard race of half-human/half-demon "giants." They even translated the Hebrew word *sons* into the Greek word for "angels" in the Alexandrine text of the Septuagint! This reveals how sure they were of their interpretation.

This is also the interpretation found in Philo, Josephus, most rabbinical writers, the Apocryphal books, and in the early Christian church. Such writers as Justin, Clement, Alexander, Tertullian, Cyprian, Ambrose, and Lactantius have this view.

There is also a strong possibility that Jude 6,7 which speaks of angels abandoning "their proper abode" and going "after strange flesh" is a reference to their liaison with women in Genesis 6. The same can be said of 2 Peter 2:4,5. Many commentators see a veiled reference to Genesis 6 because it links the fall of the angels with the wickedness that produced the Flood.

There are those who believe that the descendants of Seth were the "sons of God" referred to in Genesis 6:2 and not fallen angels. They argue that Jesus in Matthew 22:30 said that angels do not marry, hence they are not capable of sex. But it is not logical to assume that if someone is unmarried this means that they are incapable of sex. A person's marital state has no bearing on his or her sexual capability.

In addition, Jesus was specifically talking about what the good "angels in heaven" do, not what bad angels on earth can do.

The two good angels who were almost raped by the homosexuals in Sodom were evidently capable of sex (Genesis 19:5).These angels had real bodies which could be touched (verse 10). They were not ghosts or illusions. The only reason they did not get raped was because they blinded the rapists. It is assumed that if they had not done this, they would have been raped.

The objection that angels are by nature spirit-beings and hence incapable of sex is refuted by the observation that the angels who visited Abraham were able to eat solid food (Genesis 18:5-8). While angels in their spirit form cannot eat food, when they are in human form, they have mouths and stomachs by which they can eat food.

In the same way, while angels in their spirit form cannot have sex, when they are in human form, it follows that they have sexual organs by which they can have sex.

There is no biblical or logical reason to assume that fallen angels cannot "put on" human bodies that are not only sexually desirable but also capable of having sex with humans.

Hard Questions

Another common interpretation of Genesis 6:2 is that the passage simply refers to believers wedding unbelievers. This, however, leaves us with more questions than it answers.

If Genesis 6 is simply referring to mixed marriages between believers and unbelievers, why then did these marriages produce children called "Nephilim" who were "mighty men of old, men of renown"?

As we look at the mixed marriages around today, where are all the Nephilim and mighty men of renown that are born from them? The "Nephilim" are referred to as "giants" or "fallen ones." These names hardly fit the fruit of mixed marriages.

Why did males having sex with females produce "giants"? And why are the males called the "sons of God" and the women the "daughters of men"? Does that mean that no believing women married unbelieving men?

If the women were all unbelievers, it seems strange to call them "daughters of *men*." "Daughters of the devil" would be a more direct contrast since Satan had already been introduced in Genesis 3.

Doesn't the word *men* describe the origin of the women? That is, they are "of men," in other words, they come from humanity. Does this not in turn emphasize that the "sons" were *not* of "men," in other words, of this world? The literary contrast between the origins of the "daughters" and the "sons" cannot be denied.

Since the Flood was given to cleanse the earth from these marriages, it seems a little extreme to destroy the entire human race because some male descendants of Seth married some unbelieving women.

On the other hand, if the human race itself was being *mutated* as well as *mated* by demonic forces, then the Flood was needed to preserve the race as well as the faith.

There are many ancient legends in all cultures of gods or demons who came down to earth and co-habitated with human women and produced giants and monsters. This does not mean that the Bible picked up on these legends. Quite the opposite.

If such an event actually happened, we would expect to find garbled references to it in the oldest literature of humanity. No one denies that this is exactly what we find in ancient literature.

The objection that we should not argue from pagan legends and myths is usually given by those who do exactly that when they seek to prove the Flood (the story of the Flood is found in connection with the story of the "sons of men" in Genesis 6). When we look at ancient cultures around the world, we find stories of the Flood. They may be inconsistent in the details, but they are still used as proof that a catastrophic flood took place.

If such a catastrophic event as a worldwide flood took place and only eight people were left after the deluge, you would expect to find stories of it in all ancient cultures. And, when Christian scholars look for these stories, they find them throughout the entire world.

In the same way, if demons came down and mated with humans and produced half-human/half-demon mutants, this should also be found in the same literature that refers to the Flood. Scholars have found this to be so.

• • •

We have explored a broad range of abilities that demons possess. However, while fallen angels are more

powerful than human beings, they are not more powerful than the God who made them. This is why they are
doomed to ultimate failure. By understanding what
Satan and his demons are capable of today, we can
become increasingly alert to his schemes to deceive us
and draw us away from Christ.

7

A Kingdom
of Evil

There are no razor blades in the apples of God's revelation. Everything He has revealed in Scripture is necessary for our good as well as for His glory (Deuteronomy 29:29). There are no useless or dangerous portions of God's Word. As the apostle Paul said:

> All Scripture is inspired by God and profitable for teaching, for reproof, for correction, for training in righteousness; that the man of God may be adequate, equipped for every good work (2 Timothy 3:16,17)

Satan Is Not Alone

The reason you should be concerned with the subject of the demonic host is that Satan is not alone. While Satan is a limited being and can only be in one place at any one time, he rules a powerful kingdom. He has vast forces scattered throughout the whole world, doing what they can to oppose God and disrupt and disturb the people of God.

In Matthew 12:26,27, Jesus referred to Satan by the name "Beelzebub." He went on to define the devil as "the prince [literally, 'ruler' in Greek] of the demons" (Matthew 9:34). The demons are organized under the authority of Satan.

In Matthew 12:26, Jesus refers to Satan's having a kingdom when He notes that Satan is careful not to divide his kingdom but to run it as a unified organization. The devil is not so foolish as to fight against himself. Demons will not be exorcising demons. Satan will not be contradicting Satan. His kingdom is a united front governed by the same basic rules that govern kingdoms among men.

This is why in Revelation 9:11 Satan is called "Abaddon." He is the king over all the demons, and they constitute his kingdom. Thus while we may not have to worry about Satan himself coming to our house or church to bother us, he has an army of agents who can and do bother the least of the saints.

Those Who Fell with Him

Many Bible scholars believe that Revelation 12:4, which says that one-third of the stars fell from heaven, refers to the fact that one-third of the angels followed Satan in his rebellion against God.

There is nothing in the text which indicates that all of them fell at the same time. It is possible that angels have defected to Satan at different times, just as it is possible that an angel could "convert" to Satan now. There are some angels who will never fall. They are called the "chosen angels" in 1 Timothy 5:21. Just as God's elect among human beings are "protected by the power of God" (1 Peter 1:5), even so the elect angels are kept by God's power.

When the angels fell into sin, most of them were allowed to migrate to this planet and join forces with Satan. But while most of them were allowed to come to earth, 2 Peter 2:4,5 indicates that some fallen angels were thrown directly into a special hell made just for them:

> God did not spare angels when they sinned, but cast them into hell and committed them to pits of darkness, reserved for judgment; and did not spare the ancient world, but preserved Noah, a preacher of righteousness, with seven others, when He brought a flood upon the world of the ungodly.

Several things are clear from this passage. Obviously, the angels mentioned in the text are angels who committed special sins which merited special punishment. Since demons are usually said to be on earth awaiting judgment and not in hell yet (Matthew 8:29), the ones mentioned by Peter are in a special category.

They are singled out from all the other angels who fell into sin by their being thrown into a special hell called *Tartarus* in the Greek. This Greek word signifies the lowest hell, even lower than Hades. (For a fuller discussion of this word, see *Death and the Afterlife*, Bethany House Publishers.)

Tartarus is not a place where humans go at death. It is a place reserved only for certain demons. These demons were singled out for this special punishment because they evidently committed special sins. The fact that Peter links the punishment of these angels with the Flood may suggest that the sin and the punishment of these angels took place in connection with the Flood.

What sin could be so wicked that God would cast those angels who committed it into hell now instead of waiting for the Judgment Day? It may be that Peter had in mind Genesis 6, which we looked at in the previous chapter, where according to Jewish tradition fallen angels mated with human females and created a mutant race of half-demon/half-human Nephilim. This sin was so horrible that God not only threw the angels who performed these sexual acts into hell ahead of time, but He also destroyed all of humanity except for eight people!

Cartoon Theology

This is perhaps the right moment for us to return to what we have called "cartoon theology," which pictures people going to a hell (Hades) where the devil torments them with a pitchfork.

The plain truth is that not once in all of Scripture is the devil ever said to be in hell (Hades) tormenting people. The devil is always pictured as being on earth bothering the living. Thus he cannot be in hell bothering the dead.

The devil will be thrown into the lake of fire on the Day of Judgment according to both Jesus (Matthew 25:41) and John (Revelation 19:20; 20:10). Thus Satan is not *now* in Hades running around with a red suit, horns, and a Mitch Miller goatee tormenting sinners with a pitchfork! His judgment is yet to come, and when it comes he will be the one who is being tormented. He will not be in a position to torment anyone.

There is a doctrine that is currently very popular, which says that Christ's death on the cross was not enough for our salvation. According to this doctrine, Jesus had to go to hell and be tormented by the devil and his demons after his death on the cross in order to save us. This is heretical as well as biblically unfounded.

Just before Jesus died on the cross He said, "It is finished!" (John 19:30). The Greek word literally means "paid in full." Jesus made it clear that He had paid all that the law demanded in order for us to go free of its punishment. Once that debt had been paid by His suffering on the cross, no further suffering was needed. He had paid it all on Calvary's tree. This is why He was able to sit down at the right hand of the Father (Hebrews 1:3).

Since we are exploring Satan's kingdom, now is a good time to deal with a number of false ideas about the devil and his demons that have crept into our culture in various ways.

The Earth Is Not His

First, Satan likes to pretend that the Earth belongs to him. But his claim to this planet is an illegal claim. He is, in effect, a "claim jumper," someone who pretends to own someone else's property.

Some Christians think that this is Satan's world. No! This world and everything on it belongs to God (Psalm 24:1). He is the Creator of all things including the angels who later rebelled against Him.

Not Superstition

Second, demon possession is not a superstitious explanation of physical and mental illnesses. It actually happened in biblical times and it actually happens today. Because so many are claiming demon possession is not real, I've devoted the next chapter entirely to this topic.

No Ghosts in the House

Third, demons are not the ghosts, spirits, souls, or minds of people who have died but are still hanging around haunting a house because they committed suicide or have a bad conscience.

The Bible is very clear that when someone dies, he does not float around in old houses moaning and rattling chains. Hebrews 9:27 says that it is appointed unto men once to die and after that they go immediately unto judgment. In fact, they go immediately into the presence of God for judgment according to Ecclesiastes 12:7. They either remain in heaven awaiting the resurrection or they are thrown into Hades (Luke 16:19-31).

But how then do we explain all those pictures taken of "ghosts" who inhabit old houses? How can we explain objects being levitated through the air when a ghost was asked to do this? How can we explain multiple personalities, multiple voices, male and female, speaking out of someone's body?

The Scriptures tell us that those things are the manifestations of demons or of demon possession. So when a New Ager asks for a "pet" ghost, he has actually asked for a demon to come into his house.

I have a friend who did not believe that demons still exist or that demon possession still takes place. But his own experience made him change his mind.

Since he did not believe that demons were running around today, he decided to buy a "haunted" house that was selling for less than its market value. He would then pronounce it "clean" so that superstitious people would be ready to pay a good price for it. The only problem was that in this man's first and only "haunted" house, he had a real encounter with demons!

The first sign that something was definitely wrong with the house was when light bulbs unscrewed themselves from their sockets and threw themselves at him. He tried to explain this as "vibrations."

Then music filled the air even though the TV and the radio were not on. He shrugged this off by telling himself that this could be traced back to some problem with the wiring in the house.

The final straw was when a 350-pound oak chest picked itself off the floor and rushed at him. In response, he screamed, "In the name of Jesus, stop!" The chest fell down to the floor.

This last episode forced him to recognize that evidently demons do exist today, and that his house was inhabited by them.

After much prayer, he went from room to room casting out all evil spirits in the name of Jesus. In the end the house was cleansed, and he was able to sell it. But he decided that he was no longer interested in buying "haunted" houses. One was enough for him!

Not a Natural Occurrence

We must not assume that if something strange is going on in our home that it must be something natural. When my family moves into a new apartment or house, we always dedicate each room to Jesus and rid the house of any demons who might live there.

I was preaching in a church in Gloversville, New York, when the pastor mentioned to me that he and his family were experiencing strange things in the house into which they had recently moved. The children would wake up with scratches on their arms and faces. He himself had awakened one night with the sensation that someone or something was trying to kill him. He did not know what to think about these things.

I asked him if he had checked to see who lived in the house before him. Were they into drugs or the occult? Had he searched the house from top to bottom to see what these people may have left behind? Had he gone from room to room dedicating each room to Jesus and throwing out any demons who may live there?

Well, to make a long story short, he found out that the last renters had indeed been into the occult. Upon searching the attic, he found that they had left behind occult objects such as an altar made from a stolen gravestone. He then went from room to room and threw out any demons who were still living there. The end result is that he and his family never experienced any more difficulties in that house.

Other Ideas About Demons

Another idea about demons, which seems to pop up now and then in science fiction books, is that there was a race of men before Adam was created and that their souls or disincarnate minds are roaming around on the planet. But the Scriptures simply do not teach this. Adam was the first of the human race and there were no races before Adam.

Neither are demons creatures from other planets, time periods, parallel universes, the center of the earth, UFO's, or Atlantis. The Bible simply says that demons are fallen angels who have rebelled against God.

For the same reasons, it is safe to say that demons are not psychic manifestations of man's inner power of ESP. Demons are beings who exist apart from the belief or wishes of man.

Those pesky poltergeists who throw pots and pans around the room, push dishes off their shelves, open and close windows and doors, throw rocks on the roof, and turn the lights off and on are not man's psychic power going berserk. Such things do not happen because the "force" is strong in some young Jedi. The pots jump and the plates fly because a demon makes them.

• • •

Satan and his followers are fallen angels who invaded this world and are working day and night to overthrow all that is good and true. They are the enemies of God and His people. But we can and will overcome them by the blood of the Lamb and the word of our testimony (Revelation 12:11).

8

Demon
Possession

To this point we have referred only in passing to the hotly debated subject of demon possession. What is demon possession? And how can we know if we are dealing with someone who is demon possessed? These questions deserve an extended answer due to the gravity of the issue.

First of all, please forget all the horror movies you have ever seen. The heads of demon-possessed people do not spin around like toy dolls. They do not throw up green vomit or puff smoke into people's faces. Such images play well in Hollywood but not in reality.

In reality, demon possession occurs when Satan himself or when one or more of his demons enter the body of a non-Christian and take control of him, forcing that person's mind into an unconscious state. In effect, when a demon takes over someone, that demon does the thinking, speaking, and all other activities in that person's place.

This is why when the demon or demons leave someone, that person does not usually remember anything that happened during the time of possession. He does not know he was running around with a butcher knife killing people. He couldn't know because his mind had been taken over by the demon.

Can Christians Be Possessed?

I'm well aware of "deliverance" ministers who believe that Christians can be possessed by demons. Many have made an entire ministry out of casting demons out of God's people. But I have struggled long and hard over this issue for 30 years and have been forced by the biblical evidence to conclude that while Christians can be deceived, tempted, oppressed, and manipulated by demons, they cannot be possessed by them.

The first reason I say this is that there is not a single passage in the Bible which tells us that a believer can be possessed by demons. Neither is there a biblical passage which describes a Christian being possessed. Thus there is no example in Scripture of a Christian being possessed.

The burden of proof clearly rests on those who claim that such a thing can happen. And when you push them for a single text in Scripture where this is clearly taught, they always begin telling you stories of people who claimed that they were "saved" and then later demon possessed.

The fatal flaw in this method is that we are not to interpret the Bible according to experience but experience according to the Bible. Thus while our personal experiences can be used to illustrate the truths which we establish from Scripture, they must never be the basis or source of truth. The Bible alone is to be the source of our doctrines and morals.

This is why I am not convinced by someone who says that he was a demon-possessed Christian. While it is an easy thing to say, it is difficult to prove. No experience carries within itself its own explanation. It needs to be interpreted by something outside of itself.

To put it bluntly, demons *lie* because they are in the service of the "father of lies" (John 8:44). Thus we must be very careful not to assume that everything the demons tell us is true.

Contrary Passages

Second, there are several passages in the Bible which lead to the conclusion that Christians cannot be possessed.

First Corinthians 3:16,17 tells us that the body of a Christian is the "temple of God" and that God will destroy anyone who tries to destroy that temple. This passage can be applied to the demons who seek to kill the believer.

In addition, the apostle Paul states in 2 Corinthians 6:14-16 that Christ and Satan can never exist in the same place. They cannot exist in the same heart. If you are a child of God, you cannot be demon possessed.

Demons may deceive, oppress, and afflict you, but they cannot possess you because you belong to Jesus Christ, body and soul. A "demon-possessed Christian" is as impossible as a "round square." The two things are mutually exclusive by definition.

This is not to say that all those who claim to be Christians cannot be possessed by the devil. I have met a few *professing* Christians who I greatly suspected were demon possessed. But when it comes to real Christians who are truly saved, they cannot be possessed by the devil.

The Signs of Demon Possession

With regard to the signs of demon possession, the first thing that must be said is this: In many cases, there are no outward signs whatsoever that you are dealing with someone who is demon possessed. The person may be perfectly normal until they are in a situation where the demon is in danger of being thrown out; then signs will suddenly begin to appear.

Jesus' First Exorcism

The first encounter between Jesus and a demon-possessed man was in the synagogue in Capernaum (Mark 1:21-27). The passage clearly teaches several things.

First, the man attending the synagogue meeting must have looked quite normal. If he had in any way shown signs of being demon possessed, the Jews would have driven him out like they did the man in Mark 5. But to all outward appearances this man was perfectly normal.

Second, there was nothing to indicate that this person was demon possessed until he came into the presence of the King of kings. Then he became afraid of being destroyed by Jesus and acknowledged that Jesus was the Holy One of God. This passage in its context reveals that someone may be demon possessed without others knowing it.

Sometimes There Are Signs

On the other hand, there are passages in Scripture where the demon possessed do manifest themselves by their actions. The following is a summary of those signs which may at times indicate demon possession.

An Altered Personality

When there are outward manifestations of demon possession, the most significant evidence is that of an altered personality in which the person *radically* changes for the worse. Someone who was shy and withdrawn suddenly becomes very bold and aggressive. Someone who was meek becomes violent. When someone's personality changes radically for the worse, one possible cause may be demonic activity.

It is interesting to note that those who abuse drugs face the increased possibility of demon possession. The humanistic magazine *Psychology Today* sent out a survey to frequent users of marijuana. One of the questions asked was this: While using marijuana do you ever experience an altered personality in which you become anti-social and violent? Nearly 25 percent of those who responded said that while smoking marijuana they sometimes experience an altered personality in which they became violent and anti-social.

Another question was: Did you ever feel you were taken over by another personality? Again, nearly 25 percent of those who responded said that they have experienced being "taken over" by an evil personality.

The fact that pagan religions from voodoo to Native American religions use drugs to induce a trancelike state which allows demons to take them over should sound a warning to all drug abusers.

In Mark 5:1-20, we read about a demon-possessed man who had a legion of demons in him. From the context it would seem that he was originally a modest and polite man. But when the demons came upon him and possessed him, he became a very immodest man— flagrantly running around naked. He also became violent and dangerous.

When Christ set the man free from the demons, he was found clothed and in his right mind. Notice the politeness in verse 18 where he entreated the Lord to let him go with the disciples.

In terms of his natural personality this man was a modest, compliant, and gracious man. But when he became possessed, he became so violent and vicious that those who knew him previously no doubt thought, "He has changed so much that no one knows him."

Multiple Personalities

Whenever we confront a person with dual or multiple personalities, we are probably dealing with someone who is possessed by demons.

Psychiatrists attempt to deal with case histories of multiple personalities, by either denying that such a thing can happen or assuming that it is just a psychological illness. The movie *The Three Faces of Eve* is a good example of how psychiatry tries but fails to explain this phenomenon.

The "Son of Sam" serial killer is a case of multiple personalities caused by demon possession. Different voices came out of him, each taking credit for different murders. Given what he did, I have no problem believing he was demon possessed!

With multiple demonic personalities, different voices, genders, and even languages can come out of the same person.

Talking in the Third Person

Demons will sometimes talk about the person they possess as a third party. I have heard such things as, "We have rulership over *her*. We want *her*. *She* belongs to us. We will not leave *her*." When someone discusses himself in that manner, it is a sign of a potential problem.

Please do not misunderstand what I am saying. It is not wrong to talk to yourself—as long as you don't answer! David certainly talked to himself. What do you think, "Bless the LORD, O my soul" (Psalm 103:1) is all about? Talking to yourself is not the same thing as talking about yourself in the manner described above.

Talking with Demons

People can talk with demons directly and carry on an extended discussion with them. Throughout His encounters with demons, Jesus always talked directly to them. For example, in Mark 5:8, Jesus commanded them to come out of the man and then carried on an extended conversation with them.

In Acts 16:18, Paul directly addresses the demons in the fortune-teller.

Personal Violence

Very often a demon-possessed person will have suicidal and homicidal desires. This was the case with the poor man in Mark 5. He cut himself with stones. The child who often fell into the fire or water is another example (Matthew 17:15).

Demons Have Names

If you demand it of him in the name of Jesus, a demon residing in a possessed person will give you its name. In Mark 5:9, Jesus asked, "What is your name?" The demon responded, "My name is Legion; for we are many." Why did Jesus ask for its name? So that He could throw him out by that name.

The evil personality leaves when it is commanded to do so in the name of the Lord Jesus Christ. This can happen right away. Or it can take many hours. Remember what happened to the demon-possessed boy in Matthew 17:15-21? The disciples could not throw the demons out of that poor boy. Thankfully, Jesus was able to set the boy free (verse 18).

Why weren't the disciples able to set the boy free? This is exactly what the disciples asked in verse 19.

Jesus responded in verse 20 by saying, "Because of

the littleness of your faith." Some late manuscripts add the words, "This kind does not go out except by prayer and fasting." While the textual evidence is doubtful, the point is nevertheless true.

Some demons are so ingrained in a person's very spiritual fabric, that to kick them out requires a lot of work and patience. But they must leave in the end for Jesus is Victor!

Wild Emotional Swings

Long-term depression or sudden ecstatic states may also be an indication of demon possession. Remember the woman who had been oppressed by the devil for 18 years and spent all her money on doctors and wasn't any better? Jesus freed her by rebuking the demon that had her in bondage (Luke 13:10-17).

I have encountered instances in which a person suffered extreme depression to the point of being suicidal. But upon deliverance in the name of Jesus, their own personality surfaced, which revealed that they had indeed been possessed of evil spirits.

Bodily Ills

Demon possession may manifest itself in bodily afflictions as well as in an altered personality. Thus some sicknesses and disabilities may at times be the result of demonic activity and not simply natural diseases.

I am saying that *some* bodily illnesses *some* of the time *may* come from demonic activity but *not all* sickness is from the devil. Do not go "demon crazy." The Scriptures clearly make the distinction between those who are possessed of demons and those who are just physically ill.

In Mark 1:32,34, Jesus healed both those who were sick and those who were demon possessed. Evidently, demons have the ability to mimic the symptoms of valid natural physical and mental illnesses. By doing this, they avoid detection or set up a situation where they can have an occultist "heal" the sick person.

Satan can produce a counterfeit miracle by removing the illness or disability which he has already inflicted upon a person, but he can remove only what he has given in the first place. He cannot do real healing. This is the source of all the occultic healings which take place in Christian Science or in the New Age.

Supernatural Strength

Demon-possessed people are often capable of supernatural strength. Thus in Mark 5, Legion was so strong that no one could control him. When they put chains on his arms and hands, he broke them. When they put iron around his feet, he snapped it. No one could hold him down.

Once a pastor, a psychologist, and two other Christians went with Walter Martin, my former mentor, to a motel room to deal with a demon-possessed girl. Although she weighed only around 90 pounds, four grown men had great difficulty in controlling her. She would lift one or more men off the ground as they tried keep her from harm. But she was delivered in the end.

Occult Powers

Demon-possessed people often manifest occult powers and have occult knowledge. Acts 16:16-19 tells the story of a slave girl who was a fortune-teller. She was so successful that her owners got rich through her predictions.

But man does not have any natural ESP powers. There is no "divine spark" within him. People can do supernatural things only through two power sources: God or the devil.

As for God, the Bible is abundantly clear in such places as Deuteronomy 18:9-13 that He is not interested in doing parlor tricks for our entertainment. Whenever people asked to be entertained by divine miracles, they got nothing (Luke 23:8,9). On the other hand, the fortune-teller in Acts 16 is a perfect example of where occult powers originate. They come from demonic powers.

Once when I had the opportunity to visit Dr. Francis Schaeffer at his retreat in L'Abri, Switzerland, he told me what went on behind the curtain before his famous debate with Bishop Pike.

Pike was an Episcopal bishop who denied the Trinity and most other Christian doctrines. While he was a typical liberal theologian who dismissed the miracles of the Bible with the wave of his hand, he had no problem whatsoever in believing in the occult, ESP, psychic powers, ghosts, etc.! (Such "powers" ultimately led him to his death in a desert in Israel.)

After Pike's son Jim died, Pike went to mediums such as Arthur Ford to communicate with his dead son. It did not bother him in the least that the Bible declared that any attempt to communicate with the dead is "detestable to the LORD" (Deuteronomy 18:11,12).

Before they walked out to begin the debate, Pike was sharing with Schaeffer various "strange" things that happened that proved to him that he was in contact with his dead son.

In response, Schaeffer asked Pike if evil existed in this world. Pike agreed that evil existed in this world. There was no doubt about it.

Schaeffer then noted that if evil exists in this world, is it not logical to assume that it also exists in the "other" world? Just as people lie and deceive in this world, is it not possible for spirits in the next world to lie and deceive as well?

Pike was startled by the idea that evil existed in the next world just as it existed in this world. He admitted that the idea had never crossed his mind.

This is always a problem with occultists. They naively assume that if an experience is "real," then it must also be "good" and "true." But this may not be the case. Something can be real and evil at the same time.

Schaeffer went on to ask Pike on what basis he really knew that it was his dead son Jim who was talking to him. Was it not possible that a lying spirit could be deceiving him by pretending to be Jim?

This question really shook Pike because it threatened his hope that he was still in contact with his son. At that point, the debate was about to begin, and Pike escaped having to give Schaeffer a full answer.

That evil exists in the next world as well as in this world is a possibility that no one can logically deny. This is why occultists wear amulets and good luck charms and put shields and towers of protection around themselves.

There is no way they can guarantee that the messages they receive from the "other side" do not come from lying spirits! There is no way to verify who is really speaking or the truthfulness of what is said.

Vile Behavior

Demon-possessed people are capable of the most vile, indecent, and inhuman acts. Be it Legion with his crude exhibitionism or others throughout history who have raped, tortured, murdered, and even eaten their victims, their driving force or "inspiration" is satanic to the core.

Hitler and his top advisers were all occultists. They believed in astrology, fortune-telling, and reincarnation. During the Holocaust these men sanctioned the extermination of millions in gas chambers. The victims' skins were made into wallets and lamp shades; their hair into cloth; their bones into fertilizer. Such inhumanity to man reveals not only the depths of human depravity but also the activity of demonic powers.

• • •

The apostle Paul warned us in 1 Timothy 4:1, "But the Spirit explicitly says that in later times some will fall away from the faith, paying attention to deceitful spirits and doctrines of demons."

Again in 2 Timothy 4:3 the Bible tells us, "The time will come when [people] will not endure sound doctrine; but wanting to have their ears tickled, they will accumulate for themselves teachers in accordance to their own desires."

We must not put our heads into the sand and pretend that demon possession does not take place today. But neither are we to assume that everyone around us is demon possessed. Either extreme is unscriptural.

It is time for the church to awake from her slumber and to become strong in the Lord and in the power of His might: *Greater is He that is in us than he that is in the world* (1 John 4:4).

9

Setting Captives Free

Since we have already demonstrated that demon possession takes place today, it is very important to know how to deal with those who have been possessed by evil spirits. If we do not know what to do, we are going to be in big trouble.

Step #1: Make Sure You Are Saved

In Acts 19:14-16, we have an example of seven men who attempted to exorcise a demon from a man. But they had no business doing this. Why? They were not Christians! They were unbelieving Jews!

Without the proper spiritual qualifications, these seven men marched into the home of a demon-possessed man and attempted to cast the demon out. But the man overpowered them, ripped off their clothes, and drove them out of the house bruised and bleeding.

If you do not know Christ as your personal Lord and Savior, you should not attempt to deal with demons. Not only will you be powerless but you stand the chance of being possessed yourself. Fighting the devil is not a game.

Step #2: Take Authority Over Satan

You should not be afraid of Satan and his cronies. Jesus Christ has given you authority over the demonic host. In Matthew 10:1, Jesus made a startling announcement: "And having summoned His twelve disciples, He gave them authority over unclean spirits, to cast them out."

In Luke 10 the authority to cast out demons was given to the 70, showing that this authority was not just for the apostles but for all who believe in Christ. Thus when the 70 returned, they proclaimed with joy, "Lord, even the demons are subject to us in Your name" (Luke 10:17).

The apostle James said, "Submit therefore to God. Resist the devil and he will flee from you" (James 4:7). Even the humblest child of God can resist the devil in the name and power of Jesus and see him run for the hills.

In 1 Peter 5:8,9, Peter warns us that the devil goes about like a roaring lion seeking whom he may devour. But he says, "Be self-controlled and alert.... Resist him, standing firm in the faith, because you know that your brothers throughout the world are undergoing the same kind of sufferings" (NIV).

Because of our saving union with Christ, we can exercise His authority over the demonic host. Is it any wonder then that we are told in 1 John 2:13,14, that even young Christians "overcome the evil one"? Or that we can overcome the Antichrists of our day (1 John 4:3,4)?

In Revelation 12:11 John tells us how to overcome Satan. It is "by the blood of the Lamb and because of the word of [our] testimony."

Remember that you do not have any power in and of yourself to deal with Satan or evil spirits (Acts 3:12). You must call on the authority and power of the Lord

Jesus Christ. But you can only do this if you are in union with Christ.

Step #3: Get Right with God

If you have to deal with a demon-possessed person, you must get right with God (James 4:7) and filled with the Spirit (Ephesians 5:18) *before* you attempt to deal with him. You must not be in a conscious controversy with God over unconfessed sin in your life.

Please realize that I am not talking about sinless perfection. All I mean is that it is important to have a clear conscience. As far as you know, you have confessed and repented of all the sins in your life. You are in a state of forgiveness and submission and not a state of rebellion.

Step #4: Don't Go Alone

Do not try to deal with demons alone. You need to involve another Spirit-filled Christian, someone who lives a godly life, who knows how to pray, who has the right priorities in his or her spiritual life, and who knows the Word of God.

Try to get one or more of the saints to go with you. Didn't Jesus send them out two by two (Luke 10:1)? He did not send people out alone.

When the Holy Spirit wanted to send Paul on a mission, He sent him out with Barnabas. When they broke up, Paul got Silas, Mark, and others to go with him. It is wise to always go with someone.

Step #5: Talk Directly to the Demons

Speak directly to the demons and not to the person who is possessed. In Mark 1:25, and elsewhere throughout the Gospels, Jesus spoke to the demons.

Step #6: Ask the Demon His Name

Ask the demon his name just like Jesus did in Mark 5:9. Sometimes they will say "hatred," "lust," "bitterness," or "sodomy." Or they might have personal names like "Morge." But do not assume that once you have cast out that demon, the person is free. There may be more than one demon in him or her.

You must have all the names so that you can call them individually out of the person. Remember, the person is not "delivered" until you have thrown all the demons out in the name of Jesus Christ.

Step #7: Using Its Name, Cast the Demon Out

Using its name, command each demon in the name of Jesus Christ to come out of that person. One way to word it is found in Acts 16:18: "I command you in the name of Jesus Christ to come out of her."

Remember that you are not asking the demons to come out, you are *commanding* them.

Step #8: Appeal to the Power of the Blood

Use various Scripture references to the blood of Christ. We have also found it helpful to sing songs about the blood such as "Power in the Blood" or "Under the Blood of Jesus." The demons hate such songs and will leave faster if they have to hear them sung.

Step #9: Be Prepared

You must be prepared for resistance, lies, pleas, threats, a fake departure, more than one demon, arguments, cursing, blasphemy, accusations, evasions, etc.

The demon within a possessed person may say through the person, "Oh, this is wonderful. Thank God I'm free! You can go now. Your work is done!" just to fool you into thinking that it is gone. But always ask the person to confess that "Jesus Christ has come in the flesh" (1 John 4:2) and "Jesus is Lord" (1 Corinthians 12:3). Demons will not confess those things.

Be prepared for horrible blasphemy and much foul-mouthed cursing. Be prepared for lies and resistance. Most of all, be prepared for accusations against you personally. Demons will say all manner of things against you and are bound to hit some of your sins. But if they bring up some of your sins, remember that Jesus died for those sins. They are all under the blood and forgiven.

Step #10: Be Patient

Some people have so many demons and such power-ful ones that you sometimes have to spend hours or even days in which you engage in prayer and fasting in order to deal with them. I have found this to be especially true when dealing with someone who was involved in witch-craft, voodoo, or African or Brazilian spiritism. These people actively sought possession and require more time to be delivered.

In other words, there are levels of demonic powers. If you are dealing with a particularly powerful demon, it is going to take more to get him out. It is not going to be a short, easy thing.

Too many Christians think they can just say, "In the name of Jesus, get out" and everything will happen fast enough so that they can get back to their favorite TV show. It doesn't always work that way—particularly in the dark days in which we are living.

Step #11: A Solemn Warning

Once you have exorcised a demon out of a person, you must give him the warning that he must receive the Lord Jesus Christ as his Savior immediately. If he does not do this, more demons will come back and possess him and his state will be worse than it was at the beginning. Jesus gave the illustration in Matthew 12:43-45:

> Now when the unclean spirit goes out of a man, it passes through waterless places, seeking rest, and does not find it. Then it says, "I will return to my house from which I came"; and when it comes, it finds it unoccupied, swept, and put in order. Then it goes, and takes along with it seven other spirits more wicked than itself, and they go in and live there; and the last state of that man becomes worse than the first.

If an evil spirit is cast out of someone who does not go on to ask Christ into his heart, all he has done is swept his house clean and made it ready for repossession. That evil spirit will return and bring spirits more wicked than himself and that person will be in worse shape than he was at the beginning.

Step #12: Don't Touch

Lastly, you must not touch a demonic person until after you have prepared your heart spiritually and taken authority over the demons. Speak to them in the name of Jesus Christ, but do not touch them.

A missionary to Brazil told me of a time when he and several other missionaries entered the hut of a spiritist. They saw her levitating in midair! This missionary rushed up and touched the woman and was instantly knocked down unconscious. The other missionaries dragged him out. He later said that it felt like an electric shock had knocked him down. He wanted to know what had happened to him.

I told him that he should not have touched a demon-possessed person until he had gained power over it through the blood of Jesus. Throughout the Gospels and Acts, Jesus and the apostles would speak to the demon possessed, but they *never* touched them.

He checked the reference I gave him (Mark 5:1-13) and later agreed that his mistake was that he had touched her before they had taken authority over the demons through the power of Jesus.

•   •   •

These are the 12 basic rules which any child of God can use to deal with demonic powers in his home, place of work, or even in his church. We have the authority to do this because of our union with Christ.

I will never forget the privilege of hearing the late great Corrie ten Boom. She was a woman of God who literally "tramped" around the world for the Lord doing battle with demons.

One of her favorite stories was when she cast a demon out of a man in the midst of a congregation. As it left the man it shrieked, "Jesus is Victor." And that is how she got her watchword, "Jesus is Victor." To this I say, Amen!

PART II

Satan's Devices Against Christians

10

For All the Saints

Salvation, according to Romans 8, begins with "no condemnation," and ends with "no separation." This is the immutable promise of God. The apostle Paul gave us words of everlasting comfort and hope when he said:

> For I am convinced that neither death, nor life, nor angels, nor principalities, nor things present, nor things to come, nor powers, nor height, nor depth, nor any other created thing, shall be able to separate us from the love of God, which is in Christ Jesus our Lord (Romans 8:38,39).

Once a person is born again by the Holy Spirit, Satan knows that he has lost that soul to God forever and that there is absolutely nothing he can do to retrieve that soul. But Satan has always been a sore loser. Once someone comes to a saving faith in Christ, things will get rough and tough.

Since Satan cannot gain back the soul that is in union with Christ, he spends his time organizing his demonic army to utilize various devices or schemes which will keep believers in a depressed, defeated, and discouraged condition.

If he cannot get us back, he will attempt to ruin our testimony. As one country preacher put it, while the devil can never "gain" you, he will most certainly "pain" you.

Signs of the Times

Since Satan cannot get you back into his kingdom, he will do everything in his power to neutralize any effectiveness which you may have in this life. We live in a generation of self-centered Christians who are always moaning and groaning and full of self-pity. Such Christians are the worst advertisement for Christianity the world could ever possibly receive. How pleased Satan must be!

Not too many years ago, I visited an elderly Christian woman from time to time. I was hoping to hear how God had blessed her through the years and used her testimony for Christ. But far too often all I heard were complaints about her health, her children, her teeth, her aches, and her pains. If I asked her, "Mary, how are you?" she would whine, "Oh! My back hurts and my daughter is mean to me."

Now, I do not doubt that Mary was a Christian. But in her "golden" years, she had fallen into one of the snares of Satan and had ruined her testimony with her family. Her relatives did not have a very high opinion of her or her God. Her constant complaining and whining had driven them away. Being with her was too depressing!

But there was another elderly lady whom I also used to visit. She too had a lot of aches and pains. In fact, her health was much worse than that of the other lady.

When I would ask, "Margaret, how are you today?" she would always smile and often say, "Still praising Jesus, day by day!" or, "I just keep keeping on with Jesus."

I never heard a sour note out of her! When she was close to death, people came from miles around to ask how she was doing. Although she was in great pain, she said, "I'm getting ready for my graduation to up yonder, and I am going to see my Jesus."

She had a vibrant testimony in her family and in the community until the day she died. Why? Because in the midst of severe pain and health problems, she had learned to praise God.

As I grow older, I want to be that type of Christian, don't you? I want to praise the Savior and not whine and complain my way through life. I want others to be drawn toward Christ because of my testimony. This is why it is so important to understand the devices Satan uses on Christians and how to defeat them.

Disarming Satan's Traps

In Vietnam, the enemy was especially well known for making ingenious booby traps. A deserted village could be full of mines, but the soldiers would never know it. As they walked into the village, they might see a Coca-Cola can sitting on a log. If a soldier tried to lift up that can, it would probably be the last Coca-Cola he would ever have, because it would be booby-trapped.

The Christian life is much like a mine field. Satan is a master at clever booby traps, and we must learn to walk carefully:

> Be careful how you walk, not as unwise men, but as wise, making the most of your time, because the days are evil (Ephesians 5:15,16).

The Greek word translated "be careful" is the word you would use to describe the way a cat walks on top of a wall that has been imbedded with shards of jagged broken glass.

Sometimes when a wall is being built, jagged pieces of glass are scattered in the wet cement in such a way that when someone later tries to grab the top of the wall to climb over and steal what is on the other side, he will cut his hands to pieces.

No one in his right mind would dare to even get near all that broken glass. But along comes a cat. How does he walk it? Carefully! He slowly puts down each paw and avoids all the jagged shards.

This is how we must view the Christian life. One well-used scheme of Satan is to implant the naive idea that the Christian life will be easy and safe. In reality, the Christian life is "active duty" in the great war between the forces of good and evil. The enemy has scattered mines all along the way to heaven. There are a lot of crippled Christians who have had a spiritual arm or foot blown off because they did not walk carefully in order to avoid the traps set by Satan.

Some of the most dangerous mines which Satan has placed on our path are to be found in the many false teachings concerning the Christian life.

The devil inspires false teaching on how to live the Christian life in order to confuse us. Confusion has been one of his devices for a very long time. This is why there are so many conflicting doctrines on the Christian life.

Satan also inspires false teaching on the Christian life to make the Christian life unlivable. I talked to Dr. Schaeffer one day in his chalet at L'Abri. I asked him how he viewed the Christian life. He put it so beautifully that I can remember his answer to this day. He said, "Any view of the Christian life which is unlivable cannot be true. You must be able to live what you believe and believe what you live."

What Schaeffer said is practical as well as biblical. When there is a conflict between how we live and what we believe, what we believe needs to be reexamined.

The truth will always be "according to godliness" says Paul in Titus 1:1. It is the truth that sanctifies us: "Sanctify them in the truth; Thy word is truth" (John 17:17).

This is why false views of the Christian life can destroy the sincere Christian. Just as the truth leads to success in the Christian life, even so error leads to failure in life.

Dangerous Half-Truths

All false views of the Christian life can be understood as coming from one of three basic errors: legalism, lawlessness, and perfectionism.

False doctrine is seductive because it always contains some truth mixed in with all the errors. As a matter of fact, there is never a lie so dangerous as that lie which contains a lot of truth. As one wordsmith put it: A half-truth presented as a whole-truth is a non-truth.

The Burden of Legalism

Legalism is the satanic device which has Christians attempting to win God's approval on the basis of their own performance and character. God's law rather than God's grace becomes the foundation of their relationship to God. They try to live under the law.

Too many Christians think that if they have been "good," God will bless them. But if they have been "bad," He will punish them. They rise or fall in God's approval rating according to their works.

While most Christians understand that we are not saved by works but by grace, they fail to understand that God's grace is also the basis for all of the Christian life. As Paul stated in 1 Corinthians 1:30, "But by His doing you are in Christ Jesus, who became to us wisdom from God, and righteousness, and sanctification, and redemption."

The famous Dutch theologian, G.C. Berkouwer, pointed out in his masterful book, *Faith and Sanctification*, that according to 1 Corinthians 1:30, Jesus is all we need for sanctification as well as for justification. God does not save us by grace only to turn us over to works for the rest of our lives.

Human merit did not bring us into acceptance with God in the first place, and it will not bring us acceptance with God later in life. We are complete in Him according to Paul in Colossians 2:10. He is to be our all-in-all throughout all of life.

After looking to Jesus for our salvation, we must not turn away from Him to look for holiness and perfection in ourselves. Legalism always turns us away from Christ to our own personal piety or to external things as the basis of God's approval in the Christian life.

This is why some Christians are so fanatical about the length of their hair or women wearing slacks. They believe that God's approval ultimately depends on their external conformity to such things.

This also explains why some Christians are so legalistic about private devotions. If their devotions are not intense enough, long enough, or frequent enough, they abstain from taking Communion! They have turned the Lord's Supper into a reward for "good" saints. "Bad" saints must not take it. But this is the exact opposite of Jesus' purpose in instituting the Lord's Supper. It is a meal for poor sinners who, feeling their own unworthiness, know that their worthiness is to be found only in Christ's righteousness.

Paul wrote the book of Galatians because some Christians were falling into the mentality of assuming that God's approval rested on their obedience to the law. He chided them for being "bewitched" by the devil into trusting in their own works instead of God's grace:

> You foolish Galatians, who has bewitched you, before whose eyes Jesus Christ was publicly portrayed as crucified? This is the only thing I want to find out from you: did you receive the Spirit by the works of the Law, or by hearing with faith? Are you so foolish? Having begun by the Spirit, are you now being perfected by the flesh? (Galatians 3:1-3).

Paul argues throughout both Galatians and Romans that we gain the approval of God only on the basis of Christ's performance and character. Indeed, if we could please God by our works and win His approval on that basis, then Christ died in vain (Galatians 2:21).

It is Christ's righteousness that covers our sins (Philippians 3:9). We will never have any righteousness that comes from us (Isaiah 64:6). The only thing we can properly call our "own" is our sin. We must never think that we will ever arrive in that place in the Christian life where we will be so holy as not to need Jesus anymore.

Outlaws

The second basic error is lawlessness or *antinomianism*, which teaches that since we are no longer "under law," we can live like "outlaws." Those who teach this view attempt to live *without* the law just as the legalists attempt to live *under* it. They take Paul's statement in Romans 6:14, "you are not under law, but under grace," and twist it to mean that we can live as we please. One antinomian rephrased an old hymn to say:

Freed from the Law,
O happy condition;
Now I can sin and
Still have remission!

Paul emphasizes that through God's gracious act of justification we are no longer under the authority or laws of sin. In Romans 6:14, he is not referring to the law of God but to the dictates or laws of our old master, sin. This passage does not mean we are no longer under the moral standards of God's law.

The Impossibility of Sinlessness

The third error is called *sinless perfectionism.* It is the idea that we can live "above" the law by becoming sinless in this life. This view usually involves the use of some kind of spiritual gimmick by which we can obtain sinless perfection in one easy lesson.

There are many problems with the doctrine of sinless perfectionism. In a literal Greek translation of Romans 3:23, Paul states, "All have sinned and are right now falling short of the glory of God." The apostle uses a particular Greek tense in the second part of the verse which indicates that "all" are "right now falling short of the glory of God."

This means that if we accept the first part of the verse, in other words, that everybody *has* sinned, then we must also logically accept the second part of the verse, in other words, that everybody *is sinning* right now. The grammar of the Greek text cannot be ignored.

This same view of the Christian life is also taught by James who said, "For we all stumble in many ways" (James 3:2).

Once again, the grammar of the Greek text makes it absolutely clear that we all fall into sin in many different ways. James does not exempt anyone from sinning.

John, the apostle of love, was as tough as he was tender. When he encountered some "Christians" who claimed to be sinless, he rebuked them boldly in 1 John 1:8-10 and 2:4:

> If we say that we have no sin, we are deceiving ourselves, and the truth is not in us. If we confess our sins, He is faithful and righteous to forgive us our sins and cleanse us from all unrighteousness. If we say that we have not sinned, we make Him a liar, and His word is not in us (1:8-10).

> The one who says, "I have come to know Him," and does not keep His commandments, is a liar, and the truth is not in him (2:4).

First, John stated that they had "deceived" themselves. In other words, they had lied to themselves so long that they now believed their own lies!

Then he said that "the truth is not in [them]." They did not want the truth and thus did not have it in their hearts or minds. Instead, they were filled with lies.

Their claims made God into a liar because He says in the Bible that all men are sinners. Either God is a liar or the perfectionists are. It has to be one way or the other.

John goes on to say that God's Word was not in them. No one could make such a ridiculous statement as "I am now sinless" or "I am now perfect" and have God's Word operating in them.

Finally, John said that whoever claims to be a Christian and, at the same time, does not keep God's law, is a liar!

Another text that refutes the error of sinless perfectionism is Luke 11:13: "If you then, being and remaining to be evil ... " [literal Greek]. The Greek tense used by Luke clearly indicates that Jesus taught that we will have an evil nature as long as we are in this world.

A Subway Encounter

My first encounter with a "sinless" Christian was in a busy subway station in New York City. As a zealous new believer, I was passing out religious tracts in the station when one man responded that he was a Christian. I was of course thrilled to meet a "brother" in the bowels of the Big Apple.

As we talked, he stated that he had been sinless since he was saved 15 years ago. He claimed that he had not committed even one little sin in those 15 years.

Since it was a hot summer night and some of the women in the subway were wearing clothing which did not leave much to the imagination, I asked him if he ever lusted with his eyes at these women. He responded that he had to admit that he did make a "mistake" from time to time with his eyes. But "mistakes" were not the same thing as sins.

As we debated whether or not lusting after a woman was a "mistake" or a "sin," I saw that he was getting angry and losing his temper. I asked him if it was a sin to get angry and lose your temper. He agreed that it was a sin to do so.

I lifted my foot and stomped the toe of his shoe. He yelped and was getting ready to take a swing at me when I said, "Well, you may not have sinned up to this point, but you have certainly sinned now! Aren't you angry and ready to hit me?"

I will never forget the look of shock that came across his face. He turned and ran out of the station.

I do not recommend that you run around stomping "sinless" people on their toes. New Yorkers are an aggressive lot, and I was a new Christian who made a lot of mistakes. I would not stomp his foot if I had it to do over again.

But more importantly, notice that the only way this "sinless" Christian could maintain the illusion of perfection was by lowering the standard of God's Law by redefining sin so that it was reduced to a mere "mistake."

The doctrine of sinless perfectionism is a device of Satan which requires a great deal of gullibility as well as conceit. How else could someone maintain the illusion of personal perfection in such an imperfect world?

The author of Hebrews tells us that at death our spirit will be perfected as we worship before the throne of God (Hebrews 12:22,23). According to Paul, the entire sanctification of our body, soul, and spirit awaits the return of Christ (1 Thessalonians 5:23).

Another Slant on the Perfect Life

I also had the misfortune at the beginning of my academic career to attend a "victorious life" Bible college. Some of the faculty openly claimed that they had "entered into victory" and had been able to be sinless for different periods of time.

In one class, my professor was boasting that he had been sinless for up to two years at a time! I raised my hand and asked, "Could I talk with your wife for five minutes?"

He responded, "Why do you want to talk with my wife?"

I replied, "Because if you have been sinless for two years, your wife will say so. But I am willing to bet she will say that you are a sinner just like the rest of us."

The class exploded into laughter, and I got a few "thumbs up" from various students. But the professor took a dim view of me and my questions. I was eventually thrown out of that Bible college for the "sin" of asking too many questions in class.

Warts and All

One of the proofs of the inspiration of the Bible is its realism. It describes the great men and women of God who lived in biblical times as they really were. These great heroes of the faith were men and women with the same weaknesses that plague us.

It was the fashion in art at one time to omit any physical features which were deemed "unbecoming" from someone's portrait. Artists did not paint the double chins, warts, moles, or wrinkles of their clients onto the canvas. But the Bible paints the portraits of the saints of old with all their warts, moles, and wrinkles intact. You see them as they were in all their sin and weakness.

Abraham lied at the beginning of his spiritual life, and he lied at the end. Jacob was a skunk at times. Moses lost his temper. Aaron had racist attitudes. David had a problem with lust and committed murder. Paul was too hard and Barnabas too soft.

The Bible could not have been man's idea. If we had written it, we would have never recorded all the evil things the patriarchs, prophets, and apostles did. We would have presented them as "perfect" examples for us to follow, just as we have done with many Christian missionaries and fathers of the faith.

The realistic record of the lives of the heroes of the faith should give us hope. God evidently uses "crooked sticks" to draw straight lines. If He can use the likes of someone like Jacob to accomplish His will, then He can use the likes of us.

God knew that we would sin against Him before He saved us. He knew that we would be sinners in need of grace until the day we died. He knows that we will never be perfect in this life. But He loves us just the same. He accepts us just as we are.

As a matter of fact, the godlier you become, the more ungodliness you will see in your life. Like the apostle Paul, you will confess that you do what you do not want to do and what you want to do you fail to do. Even when you do something that looks pretty good, evil is present with you (Romans 7:14-25).

• • •

These then are some of the booby traps which Satan has put along the pilgrim's path to heaven. Many Christians have been maimed and crippled by these devices. All of our attempts to live *under* the law, *without* the law, or *above* the law, will always end in failure.

There are no shortcuts to holiness. It is daily obedience to God in the midst of trials that leads to spiritual growth. Therefore we must avoid any view of the Christian life which involves a "get holy quick" scheme or gimmick. Any view of the Christian life which seems too good to be true, isn't. It is a device of Satan.

11

Four
Tested Strategies

After 30 years of active ministry, it is clear to me that we are all creatures of habit—including the devil. When he finds that one of his devices is more effective than others, he will use it over and over again.

Pastors see this every day in their counseling. It doesn't take long before a young pastor realizes that he is dealing with the same problems over and over again.

Through trial and error Satan has found the most effective ways to throw believers offtrack. Remember, he has been tempting and deceiving mankind ever since the Garden of Eden and has had a lot of practice when it comes to outsmarting the average believer.

We must not think for one moment that on our own we are smarter or more powerful than the devil. If the contest were restricted to a fight between the devil and us, we would be sitting ducks. *But* (and this is a very big "but") when God saves us and the Holy Spirit indwells us, greater is He who is in us than he that is in the world (1 John 4:4).

We are not helpless as lambs before that old wicked lion. We have our armor and shield to protect us and a sharp sword to give him some good whacks. If God is for us, who is Satan to stand against us? (Romans 8:31). According to 1 John 2:13, we can "overcome the evil one."

Over the years, I have kept track of some of the more popular devices—devices that the devil uses on virtually everyone. Because they are so widely used, we will examine four of these in this chapter.

Self-Centeredness

Satan's first strategy is to get believers to be self-centered instead of Christ-centered. Too many Christians today have fallen into the trap of dwelling on themselves—their own happiness and sufferings—instead of on the Savior. If I had a dollar for every time a Christian has sat in my office in bondage to self-centeredness, I could take a vacation in the Bahamas.

The self-centeredness of the present generation of Christians is evidenced most clearly by the amount of time that the average pastor has to spend counseling his people. To put it bluntly, *too much counseling is going on*.

The function of the ministry according to the Bible is to preach the gospel, to convert the lost, and to edify the saved. These things are accomplished through the preaching of God's Word.

It is the pastor's task to turn people away from looking to themselves to looking to Christ and the things of God (2 Corinthians 5:15). This happens as the church is instructed in sound doctrine.

Paul refers to sound doctrine in 1 Timothy 1:10, 2 Timothy 4:3, Titus 1:9 and 2:1. The Greek word which is translated as "sound" is *hugiaino*, which literally means to be "healthy" in mind and body.

Why did the apostle use that particular Greek word as a description of the doctrines he preached?

When the great truths of the Bible are taught to the people in any church, they will generally become spiritually, mentally, and physically healthy. Their families will be healthy. The church will be healthy.

Good doctrinal preaching has always been healthy for individuals, families, churches, and nations. Paul tells us in Titus 1:1 that the truth leads to godliness. In John 17:17, Jesus said that it is the truth found in the Word of God that sanctifies us.

However, when large numbers of evangelical pastors stopped preaching the great doctrines of the faith and took up psychological "feel good" sermons, the health of the church plummeted. Divorce, apostasy, adultery, and wickedness have been the end results.

I have noticed that when a pastor begins preaching to the "felt needs" of people instead of addressing those things the Bible says they need to hear (i.e., sound doctrine), he unconsciously becomes a man-pleaser instead of a God-pleaser (Galatians 1:10).

This pastor will unconsciously tailor his messages to suit those who want to hear only those things which make them feel happy (2 Timothy 4:1-5). Hence, he ends up preaching popular psychology instead of biblical truth.

Once God's people become need-centered, they begin to focus on what is wrong. They begin to look inward at themselves instead of upward to their Savior.

If you go into the dark recesses of your soul armed only with the opinions of the psychologists, the sins that dwell there will rip you to shreds. You will end up in morbid introspection. But if you go into your soul with the lantern of the Word held high and the cross of Christ in front of you so that the shadow of the cross falls upon every sin you encounter, this will remind you that Christ has already paid for that sin on the cross and that He has triumphed over the devil and all his dark deeds. This is the biblical, and hence the only healthy way to examine yourself without becoming self-centered.

Instead of looking at your sins and your failures all the time, you should do what the apostle Paul did. While Paul admitted his sin (1 Timothy 1:15), he did not dwell on it. Rather, he focused his time and energy on the glory of God, the conversion of sinners, and the edification of the saints.

It is time to remind the church that we exist for the glory of God and not for our own happiness. The Westminster Catechism was right. The "chief end of man," the ultimate purpose of life, is to "glorify God and to enjoy Him forever."

Paul said, "For to me, to live is Christ" (Philippians 1:21). In other words, as long as I am alive, I have many opportunities of bringing glory to the Lord Jesus. I will serve Christ and His people until He calls me home.

Notice that Paul did *not* say, "For to me, to live is happiness." The glory of Christ is more important than personal happiness.

This is why we should never waste five minutes dwelling on whether we are happy. We should be more concerned about being holy than happy. This is the true "secret" of happiness. Happiness is a natural by-product of holiness.

This is exactly what Paul meant when he told the Thessalonians that they were his hope, joy, crown of exultation, and glory (1 Thessalonians 2:19,20). He was happy as long he saw them walking in the ways of God.

What was Paul's goal in life?

> But whatever things were gain to me, those things I have counted as loss for the sake of Christ. More than that, I count all things to be loss in view of the surpassing value of knowing Christ Jesus my Lord, for whom I have suffered the loss of all things, and

count them but rubbish in order that I may
gain Christ, and may be found in Him, not
having a righteousness of my own derived
from the Law, but that which is through
faith in Christ, the righteousness which
comes from God on the basis of faith, that I
may know Him, and the power of His resurrection and the fellowship of His sufferings,
being conformed to His death; in order that
I may attain to the resurrection from the
dead. Not that I have already obtained it, or
have already become perfect, but I press on
in order that I may lay hold of that for which
also I was laid hold of by Christ Jesus.
Brethren, I do not regard myself as having
laid hold of it yet; but one thing I do: forget-
ting what lies behind and reaching forward
to what lies ahead, I press on toward the
goal for the prize of the upward call of God in
Christ Jesus (Philippians 3:7-14).

The focus of the apostle was not on his own personal
peace, affluence, or happiness. He counted those things
as "loss" for the cause of Christ. His eyes were fixed on
Jesus—not on himself. Paul's goal in life was to serve
Christ. Nothing else mattered, not even his own happiness. This is the "secret" of a happy Christian life. You
will be truly happy only when you seek the glory of God
and the good of others.

Besetting Sins

The second trick Satan uses with Christians is that
he reminds us constantly about those sins that we commit repeatedly. He plants the thought that we are not
really saved because we so often fall into them. Hebrews
12:1,2 calls these "besetting" sins (KJV).

What does it mean when something "besets" us? What happens to a mailman when an angry dog "besets" him? The dog snarls and barks at him. It jumps up and tries to bite him. It may even maul him. It is a painful experience when a dog "besets" you. In the same way, when sins "beset" us, it is a painful experience in the Christian life. They bark and bite and make us miserable sometimes.

We have all heard the serpent hiss the following words: "You have fallen into that same old sin again! Haven't you prayed over this sin many times? Haven't you asked God to forgive you for doing this over and over again? You have cried over this sin, and now you have done it again. You know why you did it again? You are not saved. If you were saved you would have victory over this sin. So, face it, you must not be saved. You might as well go out and sin some more. It doesn't matter anymore. You are going to hell anyway."

"Besetting sins" are those character flaws in your personality that are a constant source of trouble to you. Some people have a short fuse and tend to lose their temper quicker than other people. Other people may have more patience but be constantly troubled by the sin of worry.

A Relieved Man

A downcast pastor came to see me one day. I asked him what was wrong, and he said that he was afraid that he was not really saved. He was bitter against another pastor, and although he had tried many times to forgive him, the bitterness returned. How could he be saved and still become bitter at this man?

I told him that there are sins which are consistent with a profession of faith and then there are sins which are not consistent with a profession of faith.

First Corinthians 5:9-13, 6:9,10, and Galatians 5:19-21 give us a list of sins which are inconsistent with a profession of faith. If someone is consistently living in those sins we are not to accept him or her as a fellow Christian. For example, if a man is living in adultery, he should be disciplined by the church for it. But the Bible does not say that if you are bitter you are not saved. Bitterness is not the same thing as adultery.

I then asked him if he had a problem with bitterness throughout his life. He admitted that even before he became a Christian, he often struggled with bitterness.

With great joy, I told him that all Christians have certain "besetting" sins which they may never completely vanquish in this life (Hebrews 12:1 KJV). God nowhere promised in Scripture to deliver us from ever having to deal again with this or that particular sin when He saved us. A "besetting" sin is a character flaw with which we struggle, such as impatience or melancholy, or "thought" sins such as lust or anger.

One point is very clear: *There are no instant cures for besetting sins or we would not continue to struggle with them.* They chase us like a pack of wild dogs. We may try to beat them off with spiritual sticks or use spiritual Mace. We may try every gimmick known to man to get them away from us. But, from time to time, they will catch up to us and maul us.

The Christian life is not easy. Jesus said that the way that leads to eternal life is narrow and difficult, and few people will even try it. But the way to hell is broad, wide, and velvet-lined and many people go down that path (Matthew 7:13,14).

Does this mean that when we sin we are not Christians? No. The Bible says that we all stumble in many ways (James 3:2).

Why does God allow certain sins to beset us after we're saved? First of all, besetting sins keep us humble. Every time we are tempted to be proud, the Lord reminds us of our besetting sins, whether anger, impatience, temper, greed, lust, or whatever.

Second, they help us have a higher estimation of other Christians (Philippians 2:3). When we are tempted to think that we are better than others, we can see our own besetting sins.

Third, it is important to understand our own weaknesses (Romans 12:3). Some Christians are short-tempered. Others are tempted by money. Every Christian has his own set of besetting sins. Once we know what they are, we can better deal with them.

Fourth, our besetting sins wake us up when we have gone astray in the Christian life (Romans 13:11-14). Have you ever spent a sleepless night because of a barking dog? I have. Barking dogs and crying babies are both very irritating when you are trying to sleep.

How can we tell when we are losing our spiritual way? When our besetting sins start barking and chewing us up, we awake to our true spiritual condition.

When we are walking with the King, the "dogs" stay at a distance. But when we go our own way, the "dogs" start barking and soon bite us. Then we wake up and say, "How could I have done that? I need to get right with God."

Living by Sight

Living by sight instead of by faith is a very dangerous satanic device because it casts doubt on the Word of God (2 Corinthians 5:7). This was the devil's game plan with Adam and Eve in the Garden. God told them not to eat of certain trees for their own good. If they ate of those trees, they would die. The very first device that Satan ever used on mankind was to generate doubts about the motives, character, and words of God: "Indeed, has God said, 'You shall not eat from any tree of the garden'?" (Genesis 3:1).

Satan interjected doubts into their minds. Once they entertained these doubts, he openly contradicted what God had said: "You surely shall not die!" (Genesis 3:4).

In effect he said, "Look, God is neither good nor truthful. As a matter of fact, He is lying to you because He is afraid that you will get wise to the fact that you can become a god just like Him. He says not to eat of the tree because you will die. Not so! You will not die but become gods."

Two Different Kinds of Doubts

There are two different kinds of doubts. Some doubts are good and some are bad. Some doubts center on whether or not you are a true child of God while other doubts center on whether or not the Word of God is true. There are subjective doubts about whether or not you are in the kingdom and objective doubts about Christianity and the Bible.

Subjective doubts about yourself can be spiritually healthy because they will stir you up to seek Christ afresh. It is better to go trembling all the way to heaven than it is to walk steadfastly to hell.

This is why the apostle Paul told the Corinthians to test their conversion experience (2 Corinthians 13:5). Since they had been involved in some heavy sins (2 Corinthians 12:20,21), he encouraged them to examine themselves to see if they were really saved.

Objective doubts, on the other hand, call into question the existence, character, and motives of God. These are the kinds of doubts which can bring spiritual ruin.

Doubts about God usually arise when God does not give people what they think they deserve in life. When things do not go the way they want, they get mad at God.

When we were first married, we lived in a Dutch community in New Jersey. We had a little attic apartment over the home of a Dutch woman who was the cleanest woman we had ever known. She even got down on her knees and cleaned the keyholes with a cotton swab!

When we witnessed to her, she became quite angry and said that she did not believe in God or the Bible. When we asked her why she no longer believed in God, she told us a sad story about her only daughter.

Her daughter had contracted a severe case of polio and ended up in an iron lung. The woman's husband could not handle this, so he divorced her. Our landlady had to take her daughter into her home and care for her until she died.

How could she believe in God when He did not heal her daughter in answer to her prayers? The suffering of her daughter was horrible. God should have healed her. But since He did not do so, she could no longer believe in Him.

She had fallen into the satanic device of thinking that God owed her and her daughter a long and happy life. Since her daughter's life was cut short by illness, God had failed her.

We explained to her that God did not owe her or her daughter a long, happy life. The only thing that God "owes" us is hell, for that is all we deserve. God does not exist to make us happy; we exist to make Him happy. God is not at our beck and call as if He were our servant and we His master. It is the other way around. God is our master and we are His servants.

Our landlady's unbelief was her way of getting back at God—of slapping God in the face and causing Him some pain and suffering. Her unbelief flowed from her doubts about the goodness of God and were based on the mistaken idea of what God "owed" her daughter.

All the great atheists have had some incident in their past where God "failed" to give them what they wanted or what they felt they deserved. Their unbelief was rooted in their own failed expectations.

Don't Feed the Doubts

In addition to the kind of doubts which arise when God does not cater to our beck and call, Satan can interject other doubts about God into our minds. These doubts must not be entertained by the believer. When we feed them by paying too much attention to them, they tend to breed quickly and multiply until they take over our entire mind. Rebuke them in the name of Jesus and send them back to the pit from which they came.

Romans 8:28 states that God is working together all things for His glory and the good of His people. The "all things" in the text clearly encompasses the evil as well as the good, the pleasant as well as the painful.

In 2 Corinthians 5:7, the apostle Paul said, "We walk by faith, not by sight."

As we go through life, there will be many times when Satan tempts us to doubt Romans 8:28. He brings about these doubts in one of two ways. First, he has inspired various heresies which deny that God is sovereign and which teach instead that luck and chance govern all things—including God.

Second, when we experience pain and suffering in this life and things are not going the way we want them to go, we may wonder how such things work for our good. How does the death of a child work for our good? What about rape? What about murder? What about sin?

When Job suffered the death of his children, the theft of his goods, the loss of his health, and the ruin of his marriage, he fell on his face before God and said, "Shall we indeed accept good from God and not accept adversity?" (Job 2:10).

While Job's wife cursed God, Job did not. He managed to keep his faith and trust in God when everything in his life was painful by acknowledging that God was sovereign: "I know that Thou canst do all things, and that no purpose of Thine can be thwarted" (Job 42:2).

The late Corrie ten Boom had a favorite poem she often recited when she explained how she coped with the death of her sister at the hands of the Nazis. I heard her give it so many times that I memorized it.

> My life is but a weaving
> between my Lord and me;
> I cannot choose the colors,
> He worketh steadily;
> Often times He chooseth sorrow,
> and I in foolish pride
> Forget He sees the upper
> and I the underside.
> The dark threads are needful
> in the weaver's skillful hand
> As the threads of gold and silver
> in the pattern He has planned.
> Not until the loom is silent
> and the shuttle cease to fly
> Will God unroll the canvas
> and explain the reason why.

As she began the poem, Corrie would hold up a tapestry which had a mass of disorganized colored threads woven in it. No pattern or outline could be seen.

As she finished the poem, she would turn the tapestry over and reveal threads that blended together to make a beautiful crown with different colored jewels. Her point was that the dark threads, the evil things we experience in life, are part of God's plan just as much as the good things (Proverbs 16:4).

Corrie ten Boom was right! God worked all the "bad" things which happened to her for her own good

(Romans 8:28). This is why she could say as Joseph said to the brothers who had betrayed him, "You meant evil against me, but God meant it for good" (Genesis 50:20).

The sovereignty of God enabled Corrie to cope with the death of her father and her sister and all the suffering she experienced at the hands of the Nazis. She concluded that if Joseph was able to live by faith in the sovereignty of God, then she could live by faith as well.

Faulty Self-Image

The final popular device that Satan uses to his advantage has to do with our personality. Our personality is the sum of a combination of genetic and environmental factors and the free choices we make in life. This is why we are all different. Some people are extroverts and some introverts. Some are loud and some are quiet. Some are bold and some are shy.

One of Satan's most brilliant devices is to make us feel guilty for our personality and to become dissatisfied with the personality God gave us.

The Bible never says that there is only one kind of personality that is godly or humble. The great men and women of God recorded in the Bible had different kinds of personalities. Jeremiah was known as the "weeping prophet." Isaiah was known as the "fiery prophet." Paul was aggressive, assertive, and outgoing. But Barnabas was known as the "son of compassion" and was as "soft" as Paul was "hard." There is no such thing as a perfect "Christian" personality. The body of Christ has many different types of personalities.

• • •

These are only a few of the satanic devices which cause so much unnecessary pain and suffering in the Christian life. The only way to avoid becoming entangled in them is to know what they are ahead of time.

Once you are aware of them, you can recognize them
when you fall into them. Then you can cry out to Jesus
for His help as you grow in grace.

> My little children, I am writing these things
> to you that you may not sin. And if anyone
> sins, we have an Advocate with the Father,
> Jesus Christ the righteous (1 John 2:1).

PART III

Satan's Devices Against Families, Churches, and the Nations

12

The Family Under Siege

The Christian family is under attack today as never before. In times past we could point to the lack of divorce among Bible-believing Christians as evidence of the truth and power of the gospel, but today adultery and divorce have become all too common in the body of Christ.

The devil wants to destroy the Christian family because he knows that he must neutralize the potential influence which only a godly Christian home can supply. He understands that the "hand that rocks the cradle" will rule the church as well as the world. He realizes that there is no power on earth that is greater than a godly Christian home where the mom and dad love Jesus, dedicate their children to Christ, are zealously earnest about their faith, and have a home in which there is love and discipline.

The great men and women of God in times past were often the products of great Christian homes. For this reason, Satan is very eager to destroy the family.

The Need for Sacrificial Love

One of Satan's primary schemes to destroy the family is to encourage husbands and fathers not to be an example of Christlike, sacrificial love as God commands in

145

Ephesians 5:25-31. Instead of viewing himself as God's prophet, priest, and king in the home, many men are self-centered tyrants who think that their family exists for their own personal pleasure.

The headship of the home does not mean the wife and the family exist solely for the husband's benefit. "Headship" is defined by the apostle Paul in Ephesians 5 in terms of servanthood, something that is dependent on being filled with the Spirit.

Ephesians 5:18 begins: "Do not get drunk with wine, for that is dissipation, but be filled with the Spirit." After Paul exhorts us to be "filled with the Spirit," he goes on to describe what this filling of the Spirit will mean in the interrelationships of individuals, the family, and the church. The verses from Ephesians 5:19 to Ephesians 6:9 explain what it means to be filled by the Spirit in practical everyday contexts.

The words ending with "ing," such as *speaking*, *singing*, *making melody*, *submitting*, etc., are the words Paul uses to explain how a Spirit-filled life will manifest itself.

As you read this section of Scripture, you will notice that Paul does not speak of such things as speaking in tongues, being slain in the Spirit, rolling around on the floor, or dancing in the aisles as the evidence of being filled by the Holy Spirit.

One device today that Satan has capitalized on is the idea that being filled with the Spirit is an irrational emotional experience that is somehow *separate* from the way a person lives. I am amazed at the number of people who claim to be "Spirit-filled" whose family life is ungodly.

The biblical evidence of a Spirit-filled life is personal holiness and Christlikeness. In Ephesians 5:19-21, Paul points out that a Spirit-filled Christian will be devotional in his personal life because he will sing and make melody in his heart to the Lord. He will be thankful to God for everything. In humility, he will submit to the wishes of the church instead of demanding his own way.

The word *submit* has been so abused that we should use the word *defer* or *deference* instead. To "defer in love" means that you are considerate of other people, of their plans, their feelings, and their thoughts. The good of the whole is sometimes more important than that of the parts.

After emphasizing the mutual submission or deference that should be manifested in the life of individual believers, Ephesians 5:22 to 6:4 describes what being filled with the Spirit means in the context of the family.

How can a husband know if he is filled with the Holy Spirit? Ephesians 5:25-29 says:

> Husbands, love your wives, just as Christ also loved the church and gave Himself up for her; that He might sanctify her, having cleansed her by the washing of water with the word, that He might present to Himself the church in all her glory, having no spot or wrinkle or any such thing; but that she should be holy and blameless. So husbands ought also to love their own wives as their own bodies. He who loves his own wife loves himself; for no one ever hated his own flesh, but nourishes and cherishes it, just as Christ also does the church.

It is clear from this passage that a Spirit-filled husband will manifest a sacrificial Christlike love to his family. What Christ is to the church is what the husband should be to his family.

This is where the "rubber meets the road." If a man is filled with the Spirit, he will love his wife. If he does not love his wife, then he is not Spirit-filled, no matter if he speaks in tongues or jumps up and down until he drops. Emotionalism is no substitute for practical godliness in everyday life.

But how can husbands do this? They are to follow the example of Christ in His relationship to His Bride, the church.

Jesus' Example

Christ demonstrated His love to the church through the threefold office of prophet, priest, and king. In the same way, the husband is to be God's prophet, priest, and king in the home.

A *prophet* represented God before the people. He told the people the truth that would set them free from ignorance and sin. Christ came from the throne of God in heaven to tell us the truth about God, man, the world, sin, and salvation. He is the greatest prophet who ever lived.

In the same way, the husband is to be vitally involved in teaching his family the truth about God, man, the world, sin, and salvation. He must study the Bible and find a church that follows its principles. He must be involved in guarding his family from the false teachings that abound today.

A *priest* represents the people before God. Christ is our great high priest because He gave the ultimate sacrifice for our sins and now intercedes before God on our behalf.

In the same way, the husband and father is to be God's priest in the home. He is to pray regularly for and with his family. He must sacrifice his own desires in order to provide for the spiritual needs of his family. Family devotions are his responsibility.

A *king* provides for the needs of his people. He guards them against their enemies and guides them in the way that they should go. A king is not the same thing as a tyrant.

A tyrant views the people as existing to serve his personal needs and pleasures while a true king understands that he exists for the good of his people. This is why Jesus is pictured as the servant/king in Scripture.

The husband and father is the servant/king in the family. He is to figuratively take the "towel of humility" and "wash the feet" of his family just as Jesus washed the feet of His disciples. Being the head of the family does not mean sitting around waiting for your wife and children to minister to you. It means that you recognize that you exist for their good.

Submissive Wives

The Spirit-filled life also manifests itself in wives who submit to their husbands.

Some wives are not considerate of their husband's thoughts or feelings. This is why Paul said that the women must defer in love to their husbands as to the Lord.

I once attended a church service where the pastor preached that the evidence of being filled with the Spirit was to dance up and down the aisle, shouting as you jumped. One very large woman jumped up and made her way out the pew in which I was sitting. She began to dance up and down the aisle shouting, "Glory! Glory! Glory!"

While she was doing this, her husband leaned over to me and said, "I wish that the Spirit would sometimes tell her to submit to me, just like He tells her to dance!"

The point in Ephesians 5:22 is that a wife's submission to her husband, and not "dancing in the Spirit," is the evidence of a Spirit-filled life. You may dance and shout all you want, but if you do not defer in love to your husband, you are not filled with the Holy Spirit!

God has appointed the husband to be the head of

the home. This does not mean that the husband is superior to the wife intellectually, emotionally, or in any other way.

While men and women are equal in terms of creation, fall, and redemption, they are assigned different functions, roles, and responsibilities in the home. The distinction between nature and function must be observed in order to escape the twin tyrannies of chauvinism and feminism.

Paul goes on to describe how parents, children, employees, and employers will manifest a Spirit-filled life. It is unfortunate that Paul's line of thought is cut off by the closing of Ephesians 5 and the opening of Ephesians 6.

The chapter divisions in the English Bible are not part of the original text and were in fact invented only a few centuries ago. Most of the time they are quite helpful. But now and then they cut off the author's train of thought. The average reader assumes that the author is beginning a new topic because a new chapter has begun. This is unfortunate when it obscures the meaning of a text, which is sadly true of Ephesians 5 and 6.

In the Greek text, Paul is still illustrating how we can put into practice his command in 5:18 to be filled with the Spirit. Paul first applies it to our private life in 5:19-21 and then to our married life in 5:22-33. Then the English text cuts off chapter 5 and begins chapter 6, giving the impression that Paul was finished with his practical application of what it means to be Spirit-filled.

In reality, Paul is continuing the point that he raised in 5:18 by illustrating what it means to be a Spirit-filled parent, a Spirit-filled child, a Spirit-filled employee, and a Spirit-filled employer (Ephesians 6:1-9).

Raising Godly Children

In Ephesians 6:4 we read that fathers are to train

their children in the fear and admonition of the Lord.
Paul is rephrasing Deuteronomy 6:5-9 where the fathers
were told to instill in their children a worldview that
includes God at the center. When they went to bed,
when they got up, when they walked along the way, etc.,
they were to train their children in the ways of God.

Notice that a Spirit-filled dad will be deeply concerned about the spiritual well-being of his children. He
will instruct them during special family times and pray
with them and for them faithfully.

Children should be raised to see God behind every
blade of grass. When they see a beautiful sunset, they
should immediately respond, "Oh, thank You, God, for
this beauty."

Your child should never hear from you that there is
a "secular" realm where God is deliberately left out. He
is involved in every area of our lives, and the secular/
sacred dichotomy of pagan philosophy should not be
taught in the home.

Satan hates a happy Christian home, so he has
given men the idea that the religious education of the
children is the wife's responsibility.

This is one of the most painful devices of Satan. It
robs the father and the children of great joy and trans-
fers a task to the mother that God never intended her to
bear. The father is the priest in the home, and it is his job
to teach his children until they grow up and leave.

Along these lines, another device Satan uses is the
idea that the responsibility of raising the children in the
ways of the Lord can be left to the Sunday school. This is
one reason why the Sunday school has become a point of
contention in many churches. Generally those parents
who expect the most from the church do the least in
their own home.

There is no biblical command to have Sunday
schools. Sunday school is an institution invented by

humans. While it certainly can help further the religious training of both children and adults, it should never be used as a substitute for religious training at home. Too often parents send their children to Sunday school while they themselves stay at home. When fathers are urged to give their children family devotions, they respond, "But isn't that what Sunday school is for?" These fathers are missing the privilege of teaching their own children the ways of the Lord.

Childlike Faith

In Ephesians 6:1, Paul gives us a clue as to how we can know if our children are saved. A saved child will manifest all the same things that a saved adult will manifest except on a child's level. But allowances must be made for the foolishness bound up in the heart of a child, which only time and discipline will remove (Proverbs 22:15).

If your child is filled with the Spirit of God, he or she will respect and honor you and submit to your authority as Paul commanded in Ephesians 6:1-3.

A Powerful Satanic Device

One final satanic device that has been quite effective in destroying the family is the infiltration of wicked words, deeds, attitudes, clothing, TV and radio programs, jewelry, and music into the home.

When parents allow evil to flourish in the home, it creates an ungodly atmosphere which smothers a child's thirst for the things of God and encourages a thirst for the things of this world instead.

If we neglect to raise our children to respect the Lord and His ways as Eli neglected his sons (1 Samuel 2:12-17; 3:11-14), we should not be surprised if we end up with wicked children as he did. God will not be mocked.

We will reap what we sow (Galatians 6:7). We need to maintain high standards in our homes and not let our children destroy themselves.

•   •   •

Satan uses many other devices against the family such as pornography, fornication, adultery, sodomy, abortion, infanticide, euthanasia, feminism, the occult, the New Age, the public school system, etc. But the key to overcoming all of the devil's strategies is to build a wall of godliness based upon the fear of God around our home. This alone can protect our family from the devices of Satan.

13

The Gates
of Hell

We come now to those schemes, strategies, and methods which Satan uses to disturb or to destroy churches. While Satan can never destroy the universal church, that is, the church in its entirety (Matthew 16:18), he can damage the testimony of a local church or even destroy it.

Satan has always been afraid of churches that are filled with zeal and good works. They rob him of souls and increase the kingdom and glory of Christ. This is why he seeks to neutralize or destroy churches where dedication and sacrifice are stressed and where true repentance is preached.

After 30 years of preaching in the United States and in over 27 other countries, it seems to me that there are more church fights and splits today than ever before.

During a preaching tour of Australia, New Zealand, and Fiji, I ministered to many pastors who confessed that their churches were in trouble. And in the United States, I receive more calls from pastors in distress and churches in trouble than I ever have before. As we come to the end of the twentieth century, we are witnessing a major assault of demonic forces against the local church unprecedented in church history.

Not long ago I was asked by a friend to travel to his church in central Pennsylvania on a very sad errand. He was going to resign, and he did not feel that he would be able to preach before he did so. Would I be willing to give the message just before he stood up and announced his resignation?

When I asked him why he was resigning, he described their last congregational meeting. Things had gotten so out of hand that fistfights had started in the aisle. People were screaming and throwing hymnals and Bibles at each other! He could no longer endure the anger, hatred, and fighting.

I spoke from Revelation 2:5, where Christ warned that local church that He would "remove [their] lampstand" if they did not repent of their wickedness. It was like preaching to a brick wall.

Instead of seeing tears of repentance, I saw that the people's hearts were hard. The pastor resigned, the congregation scattered, and the building was sold. The demons must have howled with glee as they had destroyed what once was a place of blessing.

Given the increasing activity in this area, let's look at some of the devices Satan uses to neutralize or to destroy a church.

False Views of the Church

Satan has inspired many false ideas of the nature and function of the New Testament church in order to get it on the wrong track. The social gospel, positive thinking, positive confession, shepherding, moral government theology, universalism, and church growth ideology are all satanic devices which have done much harm to the Christian church.

Jesus said, "I will build My church" (Matthew 16:18). The Greek text is quite emphatic that Jesus was saying, "I am going to build *My* church." Jesus was clearly emphasizing that it was *His* church that He was building and not the Jews' church or Moses' church or Peter's church or anyone else's church. He was building *His* church, *His* way, according to *His* plan, with the goals that He had in *His* mind.

Many Christians today seem to have forgotten that Jesus Christ is the Head of His church and He has instructed us in the Bible concerning the nature, offices, structure, and mission of the church. It is *His* church—not ours!

There are so many different kinds of churches today because many people do not really care what the Bible says about the nature, offices, and functions of the church. We have become so arrogant as to imagine that we know better than Christ how the church should be structured and run.

I have been in seminars where "church growth" specialists said that we can build a church any way we want, as long as it works. It no longer seems to matter that we find any support for our ideas and programs in the Scriptures. The important thing is to get the crowds into the building, get them to give their money, and get them to walk down the aisle to join the church. Numbers, money, and new buildings are the goals of many churches at the end of the twentieth century. May God have mercy on us!

That's Entertainment

One thing that Satan does in order to blunt the effectiveness of a church is to turn it into an entertainment center. In effect, people show up to watch the show that the pastor and the choir put on for them. They passively sit in their pew, watch the show, and then go home. They never learn anything. They never grow in grace. They never witness. They are content with shallow sermons that are just one long string of jokes and anecdotes.

But-ology

Another satanic device is "but-ology." Satan lets us agree that the Bible clearly teaches that the church is to be set up and run in a certain way, but he then supplies us with all the rationalizations we need to excuse our disobedience. But Christ's church should be set up and run the way Christ has directed in His Word. After all, He is still the Head of the church.

Rebellion

Disloyalty and an independent spirit among the people are devices Satan encourages to get Christians biting and devouring one another (Galatians 5:15). This is why Paul stated in Acts 20:28 that the elders set over the church as bishops were to feed and protect the flock.

Hebrews 13:17 says:

> Obey your leaders, and submit to them; for they keep watch over your souls, as those who will give an account. Let them do this with joy and not with grief, for this would be unprofitable for you.

One of the greatest problems Paul faced in his own day was a rebellious, disloyal, and independent spirit which infected such churches as Corinth and Galatia. Some people in these churches revolted against him and questioned his authority and apostleship. You can feel Paul's pain as he is forced to defend himself against all manner of gossip and slander in 2 Corinthians.

No wonder Paul said, "Admonish the unruly" (1 Thessalonians 5:14). The Greek word translated "unruly" is very interesting. When soldiers march, they are all supposed to be in a straight line. When one of them gets out of step and lifts his left foot when everyone else is lifting his right foot, you can spot him a mile away.

Of course, if the young man's mother is watching as the soldiers march by, she will exclaim, "Why look at that! All those soldiers are out of step except for my Johnny!"

In every church there seems to be a few believers who are always "out of step." They always say no when the pastor and the congregation say yes.

Paul says to rebuke them. Why? Because Satan loves to get Christians to think that they are not under any authority, that they do not have to submit to anyone but themselves.

Tongues Set on Fire

Satan also disrupts the unity of the church by such devices as lies, gossip, and slander. This is why Paul in Ephesians 4:30-32 says that the Holy Spirit is grieved when people do such things.

People use many excuses to hide their unbridled tongue. They were just "sharing a prayer concern." They "really cared for the person," and that is why they told everyone in the church what they heard from Gail who heard it from Dave who heard it from Mary who heard it from...

James 3:6 says:

> The tongue is a fire, the very world of iniquity... and sets on fire the course of our life, and is set on fire by hell.

One pastor burned out because of the "tongues set on fire" in his church. One night around 1:30 A.M., a woman he had been counseling called and begged him to go down to a local bar and talk her husband into coming home. They had had a big fight, and he left the house saying that he was leaving her. But she was sure that he was probably at a local bar getting drunk.

As a faithful and loving pastor, the minister dressed and drove to the bar. He got out and went inside and talked the man into going home for the night and coming in for counseling the next day.

What this pastor did not know was that a couple from his church was returning from visiting relatives and drove by just as he walked into the bar. They slowed down to make sure that it was their pastor and that it was his car parked in the parking lot.

The woman got on the phone the next morning and called everyone in the church to ask them to "pray for Pastor's drinking problem." He was so addicted to alcohol that he had to get up in the middle of the night and sneak into bars. They had seen it with their own eyes.

No one bothered to tell the pastor or his wife what was being said behind their backs. The gossip and the slander were painted with virtue's colors and passed around as a "prayer request."

One Sunday morning after church, a group of church members confronted the pastor and asked for his resignation. He was shocked. When he asked why he should resign, they gave him the old "Ah, you know!" routine. But he insisted that they tell him why he should resign.

One of the men finally said, "Well, Pastor, it's your drinking problem." You could have knocked the pastor down with a feather. He could not believe his ears.

He responded, "What drinking problem? I do not have the slightest idea what you are talking about."

"Ah," said the man, "it is no use hiding it. We know all about it. You have been seen time after time sneaking into bars late at night and getting drunk. It is no use denying it. We know that it is true."

The pastor argued with them that this was a lie and dug through all the gossip until he came at last to the testimony of the couple who saw him go into the bar.

The pastor had the woman who had called for his help come and testify that he had gone into the bar to fetch her husband home. She told them that he had saved her marriage.

In the end, the pastor proved his innocence, but his heart was broken by the willingness of the people to believe the worst about him after all the years he had ministered in love to them. He resigned from that church and ended up selling insurance.

Satan loves to have people disrupt the unity of the church by saying things that are not true or by saying things which are true but should have never been said in public. According to the Greek text, in Ephesians 4:29–5:2, Paul told the saints at Ephesus to stop lying and start telling the truth. He commanded them to stop gossiping and slandering each other. They were to put off all bitterness and jealousy and walk in love even as Christ walked.

The Bible says that "love covers a multitude of sins" (Proverbs 10:12; 1 Peter 4:8). If we love one another, we should let our love cover the multitude of the little sins which we all continually face.

Slander

The Greek word translated "slander" (Ephesians 4:31) is actually a form of the word *devil*. In the Greek, to slander someone means "to be diabolical." Unbridled tongues destroy more churches every year than any other device of Satan.

Satan will also divide a church by false doctrine and power struggles. This is why in Acts 20:28-31, Paul warned the elders that people in their own congregation would rise up and start teaching heresy in order to draw disciples to themselves.

In 3 John 9,10, the apostle of love rebukes a man by the name of Diotrephes who "loves to be first among them." This man opposed the apostle and all those who supported him. John did not hesitate to deal with him by name.

Every local church has had one or two Diotrepheses who think that they should control what is taught and what the church should do. Such people always show their true colors sooner or later by leading a revolt against the pastor. If they cannot find a legitimate reason to oppose him, they will make one up without the slightest pain of conscience, which must certainly delight the devil.

The Building Is Not the Church

Satan also promotes attachment to church buildings as a device to neutralize the effectiveness of Christians. The church of Christ is not to be confused with brick and mortar. The church is composed of the people who worship and work together for the glory of God.

It's difficult to have much sympathy for professing Christians who stay in a church because of the building but who complain about the terrible sermons they hear. No matter how lovely the setting, if the gospel is not preached in that building, they should obey Christ and get out as soon as possible (2 Corinthians 6:14-18).

→ If all the Bible-believing people still attending churches that no longer taught sound doctrine left those beautiful buildings and attended Bible-based churches, revival would sweep the country.

Don't Rock the Boat

Satan has inspired a spirit of compromise today which says such things as "peace at any price," "don't rock the boat," "don't make waves," "doctrine divides but love unites," "we all worship the same God anyway," "don't be so picky about doctrine."

When the people no longer care about the truth, an "anything goes" spirit takes over. This is what is so dangerous today about all the popular psychology on the airwaves. Christians are being told that doctrine does not matter. The really important thing is that they "get in touch with their feelings" and "relate" to those around them. Experience is more important than truth.

Some Christians need a backbone transplant as soon as possible! They are theological jellyfish without a bone in their entire body. They compromise the truth of Scripture to accommodate the feelings of men.

We must stand up for the truth as it is in Jesus. We need to proclaim boldly what we believe and why we believe it. We should reject the claims of anyone who says he is a Christian but who denies the inerrancy of the Scriptures and the unique attributes of God. We can stretch the words *Christian* and *evangelical* only so far before, like a rubber band, it snaps back in our faces.

Asleep at the Switch

Satan longs to see churches where the saints are so comfortable that they are spiritually asleep when it comes to dedication and sacrifice. The antidote to this device is found in Romans 13:11-14:

> And this do, knowing the time, that it is already the hour for you to awaken from sleep; for now salvation is nearer to us than when we believed. The night is almost gone, and the day is at hand. Let us therefore lay aside the deeds of darkness and put on the armor of light. Let us behave properly as in the day, not in carousing and drunkenness, not in sexual promiscuity and sensuality,

not in strife and jealousy. But put on the
Lord Jesus Christ, and make no provision
for the flesh in regard to its lusts.

If I could preach a sermon in every church in the
world next Sunday it would be, "Wake up! Wake up!
Wake up! Precious people are being lost while we are
fiddling around in our churches amusing ourselves with
worthless programs and meaningless trivia."

One of my favorite hymns was written by William
Merill (1867-1954):

Rise Up, O Men of God

Rise up, O Men of God!
Have done with lesser things;
Give heart and soul and mind and
   strength
To serve the King of kings.

Rise up, O Men of God!
The church for you doth wait,
Her strength unequal to her task;
Rise up and make her great!*

Today there are fewer and fewer zealous believers
who are sold out to Jesus Christ. Why is the love of
many growing cold? One reason is that the Me-genera-
tion has grown into adulthood and is now taking over
much of the evangelical church. People are looking
within themselves instead of looking up to Christ.

Set Your Mind Above

One last satanic device needs to be pointed out.
Christians are healthier and happier when sin and

_____
*Quoted from *The Presbyterian Outlook*.

repentance are preached and when they are told to stop dwelling on themselves and their problems and to set their minds on things above, not on the things that are on earth (Colossians 3:2).

What does it mean to set your mind on things above? Paul explains what this is in Philippians 4:8:

> Whatever is true, whatever is honorable, whatever is right, whatever is pure, whatever is lovely, whatever is of good repute, if there is any excellence and if anything worthy of praise, let your mind dwell on these things.

Why does God tell us to do this? Proverbs 23:7 tells us that we will become what we mentally dwell upon. If we dwell on evil, we will become evil. If we dwell on impurity, we will become impure. If we dwell on mental illness, we will become mentally ill.

We would all be mentally healthier if we would only submit to the Lordship of Christ and stop dwelling on our personal problems. Dwell on the things of God instead and do all things for the glory of God.

•   •   •

These are some of the devices that Satan is presently using to disrupt the unity of the church, to weaken its effectiveness, and to rob it of its testimony.

Most of the problems of the modern church would be solved if we would only acknowledge Christ as the Head of His church. Repentance and obedience is what He requires and what He graciously supplies through the work of the Spirit.

14

Disciple
All Nations

Jesus said in John 8:44 that Satan was a murderer from the beginning and that the devil is the father of all lies. Satan apparently loves the excitement of violence, death, carnage, rape, pillage, and plunder. He feeds upon hatred, fear, and violence. It is therefore no surprise that he always tries to unsettle nations with chaos, murder, and rage in order to suppress whatever righteous people are in that country.

Satan will also use politics and culture to suppress the people of God in order to bring about the destruction not only of the church but of the nation as well.

When Satan is in control of a nation, the wicked are rewarded and the righteous are punished. But such things lead to the death of that nation, as Nazi Germany and the Soviet Union demonstrate.

King Solomon said, "Righteousness exalts a nation, but sin is a disgrace to any people" (Proverbs 14:34).

Let us examine some of the popular devices which Satan is using against the nations today.

Cultural Corruption

Satan corrupts the culture and lifestyle of a nation to the point where a godly person feels out of place and uncomfortable.

The story of Lot is a good example of how the righteous suffer when the culture and nation in which they live forsakes the Lord.

> He rescued righteous Lot, oppressed by the sensual conduct of unprincipled men (for by what he saw and heard that righteous man, while living among them, felt his righteous soul tormented day after day with their lawless deeds) [2 Peter 2:7,8].

Lot was tormented by the wickedness he saw around him in Sodom. As children of God, we too should be grieved by all the wickedness in our culture. We should feel that we are pilgrims in a strange land. If we feel perfectly at home in this wicked world and are not grieved by the immorality and evil that surrounds us, something is terribly amiss in our faith.

Rejection

Jesus told us in John 15:18 not to be surprised if the world hates us because it hated Him first. In other words, if the world rejected and crucified Jesus, it is going to reject and hate us. Satan will even manipulate the media to glorify the wicked and ridicule the righteous.

Why did Jesus say to take up our cross daily? In the context of Luke 9:22,23 Christ was speaking of being rejected by men. We must pick up our cross every day because we will be "crucified" daily as we are rejected by a generation which has forgotten God.

Persecution from People

Satan incites wicked people to persecute believers. In 2 Timothy 3:12, the apostle Paul said, "And indeed, all who desire to live godly in Christ Jesus will be persecuted."

Notice that Paul does not say "*may* be persecuted" but "*will* be persecuted." When we try to live a godly life, we get into trouble. We live in an evil world. This is why in Matthew 5:10-12, Jesus said:

> Blessed are those who have been persecuted for the sake of righteousness, for theirs is the kingdom of heaven. Blessed are you when men cast insults at you, and persecute you, and say all kinds of evil against you falsely, on account of Me. Rejoice, and be glad, for your reward in heaven is great, for so they persecuted the prophets who were before you.

Jesus was always honest about the cost of following Him (Luke 14:25-35). He never promised anyone that things would be easy. He promised that life would be rough at times.

If we don't help people "count the cost" before receiving Christ, we should not be surprised that so many new believers fall away as soon as they feel the heat from their non-Christian family and friends.

In opposition to "easy believism," Barnabas and Paul went about "strengthening the souls of the disciples, encouraging them to continue in the faith, and saying, 'Through many tribulations we must enter the kingdom of God'" (Acts 14:22).

We should tell people the truth that the road to heaven is narrow and hard at times. The world, the flesh, and the devil will not stop ganging up on us until we enter heaven. Jesus gave us this sober warning in Luke 6:26: "Woe to you when all men speak well of you, for in the same way their fathers used to treat the false prophets."

If we desire to live a godly life and to stand up for the truth and not compromise our convictions, we will not be popular with everyone. We will make enemies inside and outside of the church. Those who seek to be pleasers of men and friends of the world cannot please God at the same time (Galatians 1:10; James 4:4).

Persecution from Government

Most Americans cannot imagine what it is like to live in a country where there are no human or civil rights. We have a hard time believing the reports of Christians being jailed and murdered by such Muslim countries as Saudi Arabia, Egypt, Sudan, Iran, and Nigeria.

Throughout the history of the Christian church, however, persecution by the state has been the norm and not the exception. The freedom of religion that Christians enjoy in Western countries is unique in all of history.

Too many Christians are taking their freedoms for granted and are not aware of how fast they are being taken away. Satan is stirring up the pot. The Founding Fathers of America would be shocked by the anti-religious attitude of the present legal system.

Deception

Lastly, Satan himself will come to earth one day as the Antichrist. He will persuade everyone but true Christians to worship him as God (2 Thessalonians 2:8-12).

The "Antichrist" and the "false prophet" that Scripture foretells will not call themselves by those names.

They will come not as false prophets but as fantastically "gifted" or "psychic" leaders who are filled with love toward all mankind. But they will also be able to produce fire from thin air and burn up their enemies (Revelation 13:1-18).

The coming of the Antichrist and the false prophet is the final device of Satan. He will make one last attempt to frustrate the plan of God. But he will finally learn that what Job said was true: "I know that Thou canst do all things, and that no purpose of Thine can be thwarted" (Job 42:2).

Satan will have to learn the hard way just as did King Nebuchadnezzar who confessed:

> But at the end of that period I, Nebuchadnezzar, raised my eyes toward heaven, and my reason returned to me, and I blessed the Most High and praised and honored Him who lives forever; for His dominion is an everlasting dominion, and His kingdom endures from generation to generation. And all the inhabitants of the earth are accounted as nothing, but He does according to His will in the host of heaven and among the inhabitants of the earth; and no one can ward off His hand or say to Him, "What hast Thou done?" (Daniel 4:34,35).

• • •

In these last chapters, we have covered just a few of the devices Satan uses against believers. His demons are many and his ways crafty, yet Scripture says we can overcome them by the blood of the Lord Jesus Christ and the word of our testimony (Revelation 12:11).

In 1 John 2:13, John commends the young men for overcoming the evil one; that is, the devil. This gives us good grounds to believe that we too can overcome the devices of Satan in our personal, family, church, and national life.

Satan can trouble Christians and cause a great deal of pain and suffering. But he cannot extinguish the light of the gospel of the fire of the Holy Spirit, which burns brightly within the souls of all true believers.

Even though it seems sometimes that Satan is winning the battle, he will ultimately lose this war. We can rejoice because as God's people we stand in the victory that Christ secured on the cross.

PART IV

Satan's Devices Against Non-Christians

15

Roadblocks

While Satan's strategies against Christians include discouragement from within and persecution from without, his supreme goal is to keep people from ever entering into a saving knowledge of the Lord Jesus Christ. This is why he will do everything he can do to hinder people from hearing the message of Jesus Christ.

I graduated from an inner-city high school in New York City. The crime rate was so high in the school building that each floor had its own policeman who roamed up and down the halls trying to control the drug trade and violence.

In this difficult environment, a Jewish friend came up to me and asked, "Who is this Jesus Christ you are always talking about? Was he an evil man?"

I said, "Where did you get the idea that Jesus was an evil man?"

"I hear his name used all the time when people swear. So he must have been a very evil man."

"Do you mean to tell me that you have never heard the Christian gospel?"

"I don't have the slightest idea what you're talking about."

"Are you kidding? You've never heard anything about who Jesus is?"

"I honestly don't know anything about Jesus Christ."

I was astounded. Here was someone who lived in one of the largest cities in the world, with churches on almost every corner and Christian radio and TV programs on nearly every station, but he had never heard about Jesus. We do not need to go to the Third World to meet people who have never heard of Jesus. They are living right next door to us.

It was my joy to share with my friend the good news that Jesus is the Messiah of the Jewish people. He was shocked to hear this. But as he thought about it, he said, "That would explain why people use His name in cursing. People are always cursing the Jews! So, why not curse their Messiah? It makes sense."

Millions of people just like this young New Yorker have never heard the gospel of Jesus Christ. They have never heard of Jesus and His love from a friend or neighbor! They have never watched a Christian program on TV or heard one on the radio. They have never gone to hear an evangelist like Billy Graham.

What are the typical ways that Satan hinders people from receiving the good news of Jesus Christ?

One strategy is to get Christians to neglect evangelism by encouraging believers to give more attention to material possessions than to spiritual priorities. When a Christian focuses all of his energy on the acquisition and accumulation of material possessions instead of seeking first the kingdom of God (Matthew 6:33), he loses his effectiveness as a witness for Christ.

Closely related to this is the trap of thinking that personal happiness is the goal of life, which many believers fall into. Indeed, happiness has become the great idol of our day and a great hindrance to the spread of the gospel.

I will never forget one woman who came for counseling. She complained bitterly that she was not "happy" with anything in life. She was not happy with her husband, her children, her family finances, the church, etc.

After listening to her complain for about 30 minutes, I pushed my Bible across the table to her and asked, "Where in the Bible does God ever say that happiness is to be the goal of life? If happiness were so important, surely God would tell us so in the Bible."

She could not think of a single passage in the Bible which speaks about happiness this way. Then I said to her, "If God does not think that happiness is so important, why are you so worked up about it?"

The goal of life is to glorify God—not personal happiness! As I dug a little deeper into this woman's life, I found that she was unsubmissive to her husband, she did not discipline her children, her spending habits were not under control, she was a lazy housekeeper, etc. In short, she was disobedient to God. I explained to her, "Happiness is a by-product of living an obedient life to God—one which you live for the glory of God and the good of others."

Too many Christians are sad because they are self-centered instead of Christ-centered. They have fallen for a very clever device of Satan in which he gets us to focus on our feelings instead of our faith.

You will never find happiness by looking for it. Get your eyes off yourself and onto Christ! As you do you will begin thinking of others instead of dwelling only on yourself.

Biting and Devouring Each Other

The apostle Paul chastened the Galatians for "biting and devouring one another" (Galatians 5:15), the

Corinthians for suing each other in civil court (1 Corinthians 6:1-7), and the Romans for judging each other (Romans 14:4). When Christians spend their time attacking other Christians, they not only waste precious time and energy needlessly but it gives a bad testimony to the world.

When it comes to disagreements over nonessential doctrines, the rule of Scripture is for each man to be fully persuaded in his own mind and not to judge his brother (Romans 14:5). We should agree to disagree without being disagreeable when it comes to differences of opinion.

Media Bias

The liberal bias of the media is also often used to further Satan's strategies. Christians are attacked on TV, on radio, in movies, novels, magazines, and newspapers. Hollywood always portrays Christians as wild-eyed fanatics. By ridiculing Christians, the media creates an atmosphere in which people are less willing to listen to what believers have to say.

A newspaper in my town once ran a series of cartoons attacking "right wing," white, middle-class Christians as a threat to society. Since an anti-hate law had recently been passed in the city, it seemed to me that the newspaper had broken the law by discriminating against certain Christians because of their race and creed—the newspaper used hate language and singled out only white, middle-class Christians.

I called the state office which deals with hate crimes to find someone who would deal with the newspaper cartoons. The authorities agreed that if the exact same things had been said of Jews, blacks, gays, or lesbians, they would be viewed as hate crimes and quick action would be taken. Since it was an attack on "right wing" Christians, however, it was not a hate crime but rather an exercise of free speech!

Culture Wars

Another device of Satan that is becoming increasingly popular in his attempt to prevent people from hearing the gospel is stopping missions in the name of "cultural anthropology." At least one large ecumenical organization has called for all missionaries to go home. Why? Because they are "hurting" the cultures of the people to whom they were sent!

When missionaries wanted to penetrate the Amazon jungle to reach Indians who had never heard the gospel, the government stepped in and said, in effect, "Wait a second. If you teach them the gospel, you are going to disrupt their Stone Age culture. First they'll start wearing clothes. Then they will want axes instead of stones. They will demand modern medicine. No, we cannot let you go and convert them. If you go, you will destroy their culture."

To many people, preserving a pagan culture is more important than getting the gospel to the spiritually lost souls who live in that culture. Is a culture more important than the salvation of the people who live in that culture? Shouldn't the people within a culture at least have the opportunity to decide whether and how their culture should change?

Silencing the Church

Finally, throughout church history and continuing to this day, Satan has manipulated government officials to suppress the church in order to keep people from hearing the message of salvation: Jesus was crucified by Pilate, Rome persecuted the church, Peter was crucified upside down, Paul had his head cut off, and early Christians were burned at the stake or thrown to the lions.

One of Satan's favorite tools is to use the state to suppress the church in order to prevent the open proclamation of the gospel.

•　　•　　•

These are some of the things which Satan is using at this time to hinder the spread of the gospel. We live in a time when politicians, scholars, and even some within the church are calling for a halt to missions work, when the media is biased against Christians, when Christianity is becoming more self-centered than Christ-centered. May God give us the grace to participate in the Great Commission in spite of Satan's devices.

16

What About the Heathen?

People have a natural religious desire. Satan has created pagan religions to provide counterfeit satisfaction of these natural desires. He then binds these religions to the surrounding culture, making it very difficult for someone to receive Christ in the midst of a culture that is spiritually antagonistic to Christianity.

What is God's attitude toward the non-Christians? The Bible is quite emphatic that in order to be saved someone must hear of and believe in the Lord Jesus Christ through a human instrumentality (Romans 10:13-15). Whether they live in America, Europe, or the Third World, the unsaved need to repent of their sins and to accept Jesus Christ as their personal Lord and Savior. The gospel of Christ is the only hope of salvation.

Biblical Christianity is not inclusive but exclusive. You cannot get to heaven by believing in Allah, Buddha, Ra, or some other heathen deity—no matter how sincere you are. Jesus said that He was the only way (John 14:6). Peter said that Jesus was the only name whereby we must be saved (Acts 4:12). They were either telling the truth or they were liars. There is no middle ground.

In a day when there is a strong push toward being open-minded and embracing diversity, it is no surprise to find many people teaching that it is not necessary to hear of and believe in the gospel of Christ in order to be saved. They claim that the heathen will be saved without hearing of or believing in Jesus. It does not matter if they worship Buddha, Allah, or a tree stump. This belief is known as universalism.

Such ideas do not come from Scripture but arise from the surrounding relativistic culture. Those who believe and teach such ideas have been brainwashed by the pervasive humanistic ideology that surrounds us.

Universalism can be found in either extreme or mild forms. In its extreme form, universalism teaches that everyone will be saved regardless of what they believe or how they live. This is a doctrine of demons that was condemned as a heresy by the early Christian church.

Most Christians today have enough common sense to understand that if the doctrine of universalism were true, there would be no reason or need to repent of your sins and to believe in Christ. You could go out and live like the devil and end up in heaven anyway. Missions and evangelism would not only be a waste of time and money but also a cruel joke that robs people of the sinful pleasures of life!

In its mild form, universalism teaches that anyone who is "sincere" will be saved regardless of what he or she believes. Those who teach this heresy often claim that while it does to some extent matter how you live, it really does not matter what you believe.

Some mild universalists also deny many of the distinct attributes of God, original sin, the immortality of the soul, a conscious afterlife, justification by faith in Christ, and eternal punishment.

They claim that the heathen are "saved" in some sense by believing in one thing or another. But even if they are "saved" by believing in, for example, a pagan idol, they like everyone else simply cease to exist at death. No one goes to heaven or to hell at death. They all sleep in the grave!

Unanswered Questions

On one occasion, I asked a "mild" universalist what he thought salvation meant.

He responded, "If someone sincerely believes in his religion, he will be saved."

"Do you believe that a sincere Hindu will be saved? Yes or no?" I then asked.

He replied, "Of course a sincere Hindu will be saved. God is not cruel."

I responded, "A sincere Hindu will have his wife burned alive when he dies or she will throw herself into the funeral pyre of her husband. Thus murder or suicide is what a sincere Hindu will do. Are you saying that murderers go to heaven?"

"Oh," he said, "I don't mean to say that. Well, maybe I do. Let me think for a moment."

What I was pointing out was that we cannot artificially separate what we believe from how we live. If someone is sincere in his beliefs, this will most certainly affect how he lives. To be sincere in a heathen religion may mean to commit murder, incest, rape, sodomy, bestiality, human sacrifices, suicide, cannibalism, mass murder, torture, and any number of other abominable practices.

Even though it is not popular in the anti-Christian inclusivistic culture of today to say that non-Christians are lost, "Let God be found true, though every man be found a liar" (Romans 3:4).

Some Biblical Principles

In the context of Scripture, lost sinners will not search for God on their own accord. Unless the Spirit draws them, they will run away from God as fast as they can.

Many people assume that everyone is searching for God. But God's Word tells us:

> There is none righteous, not even one; there is none who understands, there is none who seeks for God; all have turned aside, together they have become useless; there is none who does good, there is not even one (Romans 3:10-12).

By nature we are sinners who run from God the moment we are born. According to the Bible, we "go astray from birth" (Psalm 58:3).

In the Garden of Eden, after Adam and Eve sinned against God, Genesis 3:10 tells us that they ran and hid themselves from God. The sad truth is that mankind has been running and hiding ever since!

Some non-Christians will tell you that they are "searching for God." But it seems that what the non-Christian is usually saying is, "I am searching for a concept of God which I can live with while still doing what I want to do. I want a God that will not disapprove of what I do."

In one conversation with an unsaved relative, I mentioned that the Bible said that "no one seeks after God." He claimed that he was seeking for God.

I asked him, "But what kind of God are you seeking? The one true God who made you? Who is greater than you? A God who will judge you one day for your sins? A God who created hell as well as heaven?"

He replied, "Oh, no! I don't mean that kind of God. I want a God just like me! Since I would not send anyone to hell, then I want a God who would not do that either."

"Then," I replied, "you are *not* truly seeking God. You are looking for a God made in your own image."

This is the first fundamental principle as we approach the subject of pagan religions. People are running from God as fast as they can.

The second biblical principle is that heathen religions are not the result of man's search for God. They are the result of man's rejection of God.

In Romans 1:18-25, we have an analysis by the apostle Paul of the origin and nature of all pagan religions. According to the apostle, pagan religions have their origin in the rejection of the testimony of creation and in the wickedness of idolatry. He states that the heathen have exchanged the truth of God for a lie. They worship and serve created things instead of the Creator. Even though deep down they know that God exists, they suppress this truth. This is why "they are without excuse" (Romans 1:20; 2:1).

Because they have rejected the light given to all people, the heathen have been given over by God to the foolishness of their own mind. Professing themselves to be wise, they become fools by worshiping the creation instead of the Creator.

The apostle Paul does not say that pagan religions are the result of man's search for God. Rather, pagan religions are the result of man's rejection of the light of creation and conscience.

Since people believe that all religions worship the same God just under different names, the third principle concerning pagan religions is that the worship given in a pagan religion is actually given to the demons who inspired that religion and not to God.

This will come as quite a shock to many people today who assume that all religious roads lead to God. But Deuteronomy 32:15-18 says:

> He forsook God who made him, and scorned the Rock of his salvation. They made Him jealous with strange gods; with abominations they provoked Him to anger. They

> sacrificed to demons who were not God, to
> gods whom they have not known, new gods
> who came lately, whom your fathers did not
> dread. You neglected the Rock who begot
> you, and forgot the God you gave you birth.

Moses states that the worship given in heathen
religions does not go up to God but instead is a "sacrifice
to demons." "Baal" and "Molech" were not just other
names for Jehovah.

The New Testament teaches exactly the same thing:

> No, but I say that the things which the
> Gentiles sacrifice, they sacrifice to demons,
> and not to God; and I do not want you to
> become sharers in demons (1 Corinthians
> 10:20).

Moses and Paul did not say that the heathen con-
sciously worshiped demons. What they were saying is
that when the pagans worship Buddha, Zeus, Allah, or
any other god, that worship is received by the demons
who inspired that false religion. People are worshiping
demons, but they do not know it. Their worship is not
received by God but by demons.

This is why Paul goes on in 1 Corinthians 10 to
argue that Christians should not partake in pagan worship services. To put it into modern perspective, a "joint"
ecumenical worship service involving Christians and
other religions is not something Moses or Paul would
have attended. A Christian worships the one true God
while pagan religions are worshiping demons.

In Romans 1:20 we are told that the heathen are
"without excuse." This same charge is repeated in Romans
2:1. Then Paul goes on to argue in 2:2-10 that on the Day
of Judgment, no one will be able to offer any valid
excuses as to why they should not be condemned to an
eternal hell.

In this fourth biblical principle, Paul deals with the question, "What about those people who never had the opportunity to hear Scripture? Will they be condemned just like those who had the Word but did not obey it?" Paul's answer is quite straightforward:

> There is no partiality with God. For all who have sinned without the Law will also perish without the Law; and all who have sinned under the Law will be judged by the Law (Romans 2:11,12).

But if the heathen do not have access to the Law revealed in Scripture, how is it that they are condemned? Paul argues that the heathen are not left without any form of revelation. They not only have the general revelation of the creation around them (Romans 1:18-23), but they also have the general revelation of the conscience within them:

> For when Gentiles who do not have the Law do instinctively the things of the Law, these, not having the Law, are a law to themselves, in that they show the work of the Law written in their hearts, their conscience bearing witness, and their thoughts alternately accusing or else defending them, on the day when, according to my gospel, God will judge the secrets of men through Christ Jesus (Romans 2:14-16).

God has given all people the light of general revelation but many reject it.

In the end, universalists often claim that God would be unjust if He condemned those who are ignorant and sincere, making ignorance and sincerity the only two "excuses" the heathen have.

But are ignorance and sincerity valid excuses which will get the heathen "off the hook" of God's judgment? Has God ever accepted such excuses as valid?

A brief survey of biblical history will answer those questions. We'll see that neither ignorance nor sincerity ever delivered sinners from the wrath of God.

A Survey of History

Jesus said that the Judgment Day will be patterned after what happened at the Flood (Matthew 24:39). Were there any ignorant and sincere people in Noah's day? Of course there were. People are people regardless of when they live.

Did God bring all the ignorant and sincere people into the ark? No. What happened to these ignorant and sincere people? They perished under the judgment of God.

The only ones who were saved from the flood of God's wrath were those who heard of and believed in the preaching of Noah. The ark was exclusive and not inclusive.

The Judgment Day will also be patterned after what happened at Sodom and Gomorrah according to 2 Peter 2:6. Were there any sincere and ignorant people in those cities? Yes. Did the angels come and deliver them from the fire of God's wrath? No. They perished.

The only ones who were saved from the fire were the ones who heard of and believed in Lot's message. Again, salvation was exclusive and not inclusive.

There were sincere and ignorant Egyptians in Moses' day, but neither sincerity nor ignorance delivered them from the plagues. They suffered just as much as the insincere and those who knowingly rejected God's Word.

Whose firstborn escaped the angel of death? Only those who heard of and believed in the message of Moses. It was clearly exclusive and not inclusive.

There were sincere and ignorant Canaanites in Jericho, but they too perished. Rahab and her family alone escaped the destruction of Jericho. How did they escape the judgment of God? Whoever heard and believed in the message of Rahab was saved. Everyone else died. Deliverance was exclusive and not inclusive.

As we go through redemptive history, every example of salvation is exclusive and not inclusive. We must hear and believe in God's Word in order to be saved. Ignorance and sincerity never at any time under any circumstance delivered anyone from the judgment of God.

This is exactly the point that Jesus made in Luke 12:47,48. Just because the slave was ignorant of his master's will did not deliver him from punishment. Ignorance was no excuse.

This same thing can be said of 2 Thessalonians 1:8 where Paul says that ignorance of God is the basis of divine judgment. Every attempt to turn the very basis of divine judgment into an excuse to escape it is completely unfounded.

How Shall They Hear?

The fifth principle naturally flows from the fourth principle: Lost sinners must hear of and believe in the gospel of Christ in order to be saved.

This was the experience of Cornelius as recorded in the book of Acts. Although he was a Gentile convert to Judaism (Acts 10:2), and he was a sincere and good man, he was not yet "saved" according to Acts 11:14 because he had not heard of and believed in Jesus.

The angel told Cornelius to send for Peter so that he could hear and believe in his message. If he believed what Peter told him, he would be saved. And if his family also heard and believed, they too would be saved.

Notice that the angel did not preach the gospel to

Cornelius. Angels were not given the Great Commission. Redeemed humanity has been given the glorious task of preaching the gospel.

What is so important about this passage is that the sincerity and ignorance of Cornelius did not save him. He had to hear the gospel through a human instrumentality in order to be saved.

We not only have the example of Cornelius, but we also have the clear doctrinal statement of Paul in Romans 10:9-17. This passage has always been the sword which cuts off the head of the serpent of universalism.

> If you confess with your mouth Jesus as Lord, and believe in your heart that God raised Him from the dead, you shall be saved...for "Whoever will call upon the name of the Lord will be saved." How then shall they call upon Him in whom they have not believed? And how shall they believe in Him whom they have not heard? And how shall they hear without a preacher? And how shall they preach unless they are sent? ...So faith comes from hearing, and hearing by the word of Christ.

The words of Paul could not be any clearer. In order to be saved, a sinner must hear of and believe in the "word of Christ" which is synonymous for the gospel. The logic is simple and straightforward.

Put another way:

> If no one preaches Christ to you,
>   then you cannot hear of Him.
> If you cannot hear of Christ,
>   then you cannot believe in Him.
> If you cannot believe in Him,
>   then you cannot be saved.

If someone preaches Christ to you,
> then you will hear of Him.
If you hear of Christ,
> then you can believe in Him.
If you believe in Christ,
> then you will be saved.

•   •   •

Who are the heathen? Anyone who is not saved is a heathen. Unbelievers here at home or in foreign lands need Christ. This is why missionaries must be sent to foreign lands as well as to our own nation. The heathen are perishing in their sins. Jesus is the Only Way.

17

Excuses, Excuses

Satan has planted, nurtured, and encouraged various excuses over the years which many people use to justify their refusal to become a Christian. These excuses may appeal to man's willful nature, but they do not change God's plan of salvation, which is through faith in Christ alone.

Let's examine some of these excuses.

Excuse #1:
There Is No God

There is no God, no life after death, and no moral absolutes. Eat, drink, and be merry because we will all die and pass into noth- ingness.

This was my father's great hope. Whenever I would witness to him, he would tell me, "I know this guy who died, but they opened his chest and massaged his heart and he came back to life. I asked him what he saw after death. He said, 'I did not see anything at all. There was no heaven or hell.' So, don't tell me that when I die there is a hell. There is nothing but the grave."

I responded that such stories don't prove or disprove the afterlife. "I can match you story for story of people who saw heaven or hell after they 'died' according to your definition. But I don't believe these people died in the true sense of the word. Death is more than the cessation of a heartbeat."

When my father himself lay dying, I was able to witness to him once again and this time around I believe he repented of his unbelief and accepted Christ.

Psalm 14:1 says, "The fool has said in his heart, 'There is no God.'" Why is it foolish to believe that God doesn't exist? Because a person would have to know all things and be everywhere at the same time through all of time past, present, and future in order to say with certainty that there is no God. No one can do that but God, and He is certainly not an atheist.

Occasionally I have challenged people who deny the existence of God by saying, "If the Bible is right, you will go to hell. But I will go to heaven. If on the other hand, the Bible is wrong, I will have lived a happy life because I thought my sins were forgiven and I believed I was going to heaven. But you will have found no meaning in life and no ultimate destiny of which you are assured. So if the Bible is right you lose, and if the Bible is wrong you lose. The Christian wins either way."

I have done this to help people think through the consequences of their choices. As yet no one has offered a reasonable answer to this "quality of life" challenge.

Excuse #2:
All Religions Are Equally True

All religions are the same. Everyone actually worships the same God just under different names. As long as you are sincere, it doesn't matter what you believe. Everyone goes to heaven when they die. There is no hell.

In John 3:16, Jesus said that the only way we can keep from perishing is to believe in Him: "For God so loved the world, that He gave His only begotten Son, that whoever believes in Him should not perish, but have eternal life."

In John 14:6, Jesus said, "I am the way, and the truth, and the life; no one comes to the Father, but through Me."

Jesus is not *a* way. He is *the* way. He is the only way to the Father.

The apostle Peter in Acts 4:12 said, "There is no other name under heaven that has been given among men, by which we must be saved."

We've gone into detail about this in an earlier chapter, but it doesn't hurt to repeat the point: We must hear of and believe in the Lord Jesus Christ to be saved. The name of Buddha, Muhammad, Krishna, Reverend Moon, or a sacred crocodile will never save anyone from his or her sins.

The Example of the Jailer

Acts 16:30,31 offers a perfect example of the exclusive nature of Christianity. In this passage Paul's jailer asks, "What must I do to be saved?" Paul didn't tell the jailer, "Well, just be sincere in your own religious belief. That is how you can be saved. By the way, what do you believe in?"

"Ah, I worship Diana of Ephesus."

"Well, as long as you are sincere in worshiping Diana of Ephesus, you will be saved."

Is that what Paul said to the jailer? Not at all. He said, "Believe in the Lord Jesus, and you shall be saved."

If the jailer did not believe, he would not be saved.

In 1 Timothy 2:5, we are told, "There is...one mediator...between God and man, the man Christ Jesus."

A mediator is a go-between, someone who represents two opposite sides. The task of a mediator is to bring the two sides together. Because Jesus Christ alone can bring together man and God through His atoning work on the cross, He is the only mediator. No other mediator will do.

I was speaking on a TV talk show when the host angrily confronted me. He said, "How unkind you are to say that Christianity is the only religion! All religions worship the same God, only under different names. Don't you know that the Bible says not to judge other people? How dare you judge other religions?"

I responded, "If you really believed a person should not judge other people or other religions, why then are you judging me and my religion? If truth is relative, as you suggest, then you have no right to say that my religion is false."

Many people use a double standard when it comes to Christians. They try to say "every religion is true" and "Christianity is false" at the same time! We must in love point out that they are contradicting themselves.

But what about Jesus' words: "Do not judge lest you be judged" (Matthew 7:1)? How can we as Christians judge other religions as wrong or judge people as sinners and still follow what Jesus taught?

The idea that we should not judge anything is a satanic device that would lead us to affirm all the evil around us. To be completely nonjudgmental is to fall into the snare of the evil one.

When Jesus spoke these words, He was not forbidding His disciples to judge people. He was actually rebuking the hypocrites in the audience who condemned people publicly for sins they themselves were committing in secret. This is why in Matthew 7:5 Jesus identifies the one He is rebuking by saying, "You hypocrite."

When He addressed His faithful disciples in the

same sermon, Jesus told them to judge certain people as
"swine" and "dogs" (verse 6) and label them as "false
prophets" (verses 15-20). By their fruits the disciples
would be able to know and judge these types of hypocrites.

Another time Jesus said to His disciples, "Judge
with righteous judgment" (John 7:24). We are to judge
people according to the Word of God. After all, sinners
would not be evangelized if we did not first consider
them lost. People would not be baptized if we did not
consider them saved. People could not be disciplined by
the church if we did not consider them guilty of sin. As a
matter of fact, according to 1 Corinthians 6:2, the saints
will judge the world. In order to obey Jesus' command in
John 7:24, we must judge people by the doctrines and
morals of Scriptures.

Excuse #3:
People Are Basically Good

*People are basically good. Man is not a sin-
ner by nature. He does evil things because of
his ignorance or environment.*

The Bible and human experience give abundant
proof of the depravity of man. What parent has had to
teach his children to lie or steal? We sin because we are
sinners by nature, according to Paul in Romans 5:16-20.
Paul also said, "All have sinned and fall short of the
glory of God" (Romans 3:23).

The Keys Ring in the Truth

As I drove a friend of the family to New York City, I
took the opportunity to witness to her. When I told her
that she needed to repent of her sins and turn to Christ,
she surprised me by saying that she did not have any

sins to repent of. According to her, evil, or sin, did not really exist. She said, "All was God and God was good. Thus all is good and there is no evil."

The Lord quietly gave me a wonderful way to illustrate the reality of evil. I asked my friend to reach into her purse and get out her keys. She reached in and brought out a key ring with about ten keys on it.

I took the key ring and began rattling the keys. As they clinked and clanked, she said, "Why are you doing that?" I said, "To get your attention. If you really believed that evil does not exist and that all people are innately good, why do you lock your apartment? Your car? Your office? If there is no such thing as evil, leave everything unlocked! And then I will drop you off in the inner city tonight around midnight. I don't think it will take long to discover that evil does exist."

Evil does exist and so do evil people. To believe otherwise is to be blind to the realities of life.

Excuse #4:
I Want to Have Some Fun First

Don't worry. I will be saved one day. But I want to have some fun first.

If you work with young people, you already know that this is one device that Satan uses all the time. Satan tells young people that they have plenty of time to repent. No need to rush the decision to receive Christ. They have their whole lives ahead of them.

In truth God hasn't promised *anyone* all the time in the world to repent. He hasn't even promised them the next five minutes. Young people die. Old people die. Children die. We're all just a moment away from eternity. This is why 2 Corinthians 6:2 says, "Behold, now is 'the acceptable time,' behold, now is 'the day of salvation.'"

Excuse #5:
Wicked People Have More Fun

People who live for themselves have a happier life than those who live for God. Look around you. Who are the rich? The powerful? The beautiful? They are the ones who look out for their own interests. Christians are losers.

In Psalm 73, Asaph confessed that at one time in his life, he became envious of wicked rich people who seemed happier than he was. They seemed to have everything going their way. They didn't have to worry about money like he did. They could buy whatever they wanted. Go wherever they wanted. They lived a life of ease. On the other hand, the life of the believer is often hard. He is mocked by those around him. He is often hard up for money. He grieves over his own sins and the sins of those around him. He refrains from the sinful pleasures of life.

Asaph found out the truth when he went into the temple and had a talk with God:

> Surely Thou dost set them in slippery places; Thou dost cast them down to destruction. How they are destroyed in a moment! They are utterly swept away by sudden terrors! Like a dream when one awakes, O Lord, when aroused, Thou wilt despise their form (Psalm 73:18-20).

Surely, God had put the feet of the wicked on slippery places. Riches tend to destruction. The love of money is the root of all evil. Once Asaph considered that the wicked ended up in hell regardless of how much money they had, the sinful pleasures of this life did not look so appealing.

Excuse #6:
The Church Is Filled with Hypocrites

Look at all the hypocrites in the church!
Don't talk to me about becoming a Christian.
I know all I want to know about Christians.
They are all hypocrites.

This device of Satan has been on the Top 10 Excuses list for years. In order to counter it successfully, consider the following.

First, the center of Christianity is Christ Himself, not Christians. Was Jesus a hypocrite? To judge the truth of Christianity by the failures of those who claim to follow Christ is like judging Mozart's music by a violin student's first recital.

Corrie ten Boom said on one occasion that while she was able to forgive the Nazis who murdered her sister, she found it incredibly difficult to forgive Christians who had sinned against her.

I have discovered the same thing. Christians know better than to act unbecomingly, and so have no excuse. This is why it is harder to forgive them.

Second, Christians are people too. If a Christian has annoying personality traits before he is saved, he will probably still have some of them afterward to a degree.

Third, not all hypocrites are Christians. You can find hypocrites in schools, offices, and every type of organization. In order to escape being with hypocrites, you would have to live in a cave or fly to the moon.

Fourth, the Bible says that all hypocrites—those people who do not live what they profess—will be thrown into hell (Matthew 24:51). If we neglect salvation because there are some hypocrites in the church, then we will most surely end up in hell with them for all eternity!

Excuse #7:
My Family Wouldn't Approve

My family would disown me if I became a
Christian. How can I turn my back on what
my parents have taught me?

The pull of the family is hard to overcome. Yet there are times when we must choose between our family and our God. In Matthew 10:32-39, Jesus said that our relationship to Him must have ultimate priority over all other relationships. The Lord Jesus Christ must mean more to us then our mother, father, brother, sister, husband, wife, children, grandchildren, aunts, uncles, or anybody else.

I know the pain of having to give up my family for Christ. After my conversion to Christ, my father gave me an ultimatum: Leave Jesus or leave home. The choice was hard but clear. I left my home not knowing how or where I would live. Jesus meant more to me than my own family. And He took care of me all the years I worked my way through college and seminary. He was always faithful, though I was unfaithful many times.

Excuse #8:
I Don't Need a Savior

Why should I become a Christian? I have
everything under control. I don't need a sav-
ior. I can handle things all right. I don't feel
any need for Jesus. I am happy the way I am.
If you need Christianity, great! But don't
push it on me. I don't need it.

Surprising numbers of people today feel that they do not need salvation. This feeling is a very powerful device Satan uses to hinder sinners from seeking the Savior.

The "I'm OK—you're OK" and "believe in yourself" psychologies of the 1980s have created an entire generation of people who think that they do not need anyone or anything outside of themselves. This is of course the essence of the New Age Movement, which tells us to look to the "divine higher self" within for all that we need in life.

On one occasion during a live call-in radio show, a New Ager told me that she did not need Jesus. I responded by asking her if she or a loved one had ever had a serious illness. She did not answer my question but tried to change the topic.

After some persistence, she finally admitted that she did have a loved one who had suffered a serious illness.

I asked her if she had prayed for her loved one to get well. She hesitated for a moment and then admitted that she had prayed that way for her grandmother.

"Then you do not have all you need within yourself," I said. "When the rubber met the road, you had to go outside of yourself and ask God to heal your grandmother. New Age thinking 'works' as long as everything is fine. But life is full of surprises, and you will eventually find that you need a savior."

Many people are like this woman. As long as things are going their way, they think that they do not need God. But when the trials of life come, they find that they do not have all that they need inside of themselves.

Excuse #9:
I Am a Good Person

I was born into a Christian home. I am baptized and a church member. I am a good person. What else would God demand?

Millions of people trust in their own deeds of love and kindness to get them to heaven. They assume that

God will accept them on the basis of their character and the nature of their performance.

Shortly before he died of cancer, the famous actor John Wayne was interviewed on TV. During the interview, he was asked, "Are you ready to meet your Maker?"

I sat in front of the TV hoping against hope that he would indicate in some way that he placed his hopes for heaven on Christ. But I was disappointed. The Duke replied that the "Man Upstairs" would take into consideration the good things he had done as well as the bad. He was sure that his good deeds outweighed his bad deeds and that he would go to heaven when he died.

We are not saved on the basis of being born into a Christian home, baptism, church membership, or good works (Titus 3:5). We are saved on the basis of the person and work of Jesus Christ. This is why salvation is by *grace alone* through *faith alone* in *Christ alone* (Ephesians 2:8,9). There is no other way to heaven.

Excuse #10:
I'm Just a Carnal Christian

I received Christ as my Savior years ago. I may not be one of those super-duper Christians but I'm saved anyway. I am just a carnal Christian. And I am content to receive a small reward on the Judgment Day.

Of all the devices of Satan, this perhaps destroys more souls then any other. Millions of people think that they are carnal Christians who are saved. That they are "carnal" is all too true. But that they are Christians is not true.

Many people show up in churches on Sunday mornings because of motivations other than "hungering and thirsting after righteousness." They come to please their wife or husband. They come to hear a good speaker.

They come because they were raised in that church. They come for many reasons, but the bottom line is always the same: They are not committed to living life in obedience to the Lord Jesus Christ. Their profession of faith is an empty one. They have never really moved from professing salvation to possessing salvation.

Jesus described individuals like this in Matthew 7:21: "Not everyone who says to Me, 'Lord, Lord,' will enter the kingdom of heaven; but he who does the will of My Father who is in heaven."

And what happens to those people who fail to do the will of the Father? Jesus says in verse 23: "And then I will declare to them, 'I never knew you; depart from Me, you who practice lawlessness.'"

This may seem harsh to some people, particularly to "carnal" Christians! But I am not saying anything that is not taught in the New Testament. The apostle John called the carnal Christians of his day "liars": "The one who says, 'I have come to know Him,' and does not keep His commandments, is a liar, and the truth is not in him" (1 John 2:4).

John, the "apostle of love," did not pussyfoot around with those whose walk did not equal their talk. He openly challenged anyone who claimed to be a Christian but whose life was a contradiction of that claim.

This same bold approach was taken by the apostle Paul. In 1 Corinthians 5:9-13, he commands the Corinthians not to associate with any so-called brother who is an "immoral person, or covetous, or an idolater, or a reviler, or a drunkard, or a swindler." We are not to even sit down and eat a meal with him.

Paul tells us to judge those within the visible church who are carnal (1 Corinthians 5:12). And Paul was not asking us to do something that he himself did not do.

When confronted with the report of a young man who was sexually involved with his stepmother, Paul "judged" the man guilty: "For I, on my part, though absent in body but present in spirit, have already judged him who has so committed this, as though I were present" (1 Corinthians 5:3).

He went on to put teeth in this judgment by commanding the congregation to excommunicate the young man (1 Corinthians 5:4,5).

In Romans 8:6, Paul tells us that to be "carnal" means death. Then he goes on in verse 7 to say that "the mind set on the flesh ... does not subject itself to the law of God, for it is not even able to do so."

In 2 Corinthians 5:17, we are told that, "Therefore if any man is in Christ, he is a new creature; the old things passed away; behold, new things have come."

What the apostle was saying was that when someone is truly regenerated by the Spirit of God, there is a radical change in the way he thinks, feels, and acts. In other words, he is no longer "carnal" in his thoughts, words, and deeds. He is now "spiritual."

This radical change is signified by Paul's choice of wording. The old way of living has "passed away" and a new way of living "has come." The grammar of the passage emphasizes the radical nature of regeneration.

This is why Paul tells his readers not to be deceived by people who claim to be saved and yet do not live like it. He gives the sober warning that they who live carnally shall not inherit the kingdom of God (1 Corinthians 6:9,10; cf. Galatians 5:19-21).

A well-versed carnal Christian will respond by asking, "But what about the Corinthians? Weren't they carnal Christians?"

In truth, the Corinthians actually strengthen the point that the salvation of anyone whose life is "carnal" is suspect.

The Corinthians were acting "carnally" by engaging in "strife, jealousy, angry tempers, disputes, slanders, gossip, arrogance, disturbances ... impurity, immorality and sensuality" (2 Corinthians 12:20,21). This prompts

Paul to admonish them: "Test yourselves to see if you
are in the faith; examine yourselves!" (2 Corinthians
13:5).

He warns them:

> Do you not know that the unrighteous shall
> not inherit the kingdom of God? Do not be
> deceived; neither fornicators, nor idolaters,
> nor adulterers, nor effeminate, nor homo-
> sexuals, nor thieves, nor the covetous, nor
> drunkards, nor revilers, nor swindlers, shall
> inherit the kingdom of God (1 Corinthians
> 6:9,10).

When Paul complained in 1 Corinthians 3:1-4 that
the Corinthians were acting like carnal men, he was
saying that they were acting like unregenerate sinners.
(He had already contrasted the term *natural* to the word
spiritual in 1 Corinthians 2:14,15 to make a clear distinction between the saved and the lost.)

But what about the rewards mentioned in 1 Corinthians 3:9-15? Paul is not saying that "carnal" Christians will be saved although they will have few rewards.
The passage clearly has evangelists and pastors in focus
and refers to the gain or loss of rewards in the Christian
ministry.

On the Day of Judgment, the ministry of each
pastor, evangelist, and teacher will be tested to see how
faithfully it has been executed. Since this is a test of
one's ministry and not one's salvation, it is conceivable
that some pastors will be saved but see their life's work
go up in flames because it was not founded on the Rock,
Christ Jesus.

Easy Believism

Closely related to the carnal Christian is the person

whom Satan has deceived into thinking that true saving faith is simply an intellectual assent to the facts of the gospel. As long as they "believe" that Jesus is the Christ, they assume that they are saved.

Even though they are Protestants, they have unconsciously accepted the Roman Catholic view of faith—that salvation comes to those who give intellectual assent to the doctrines of the Catholic Church. It is not necessary to understand what those doctrines mean. It is not even necessary to accept Christ as your personal Savior. All you have to do is to assent to the teachings of the Church as true.

At the time of the Reformation, Calvin and the other Reformers clearly saw that true saving faith is *more* than a mere intellectual assent to doctrine. True saving faith is made up of three things:

- a knowledge of the gospel
- an intellectual assent to its truthfulness
- a personal commitment to Christ

If we do not know what the gospel teaches, we cannot assent to its truth. But there is one more step to true saving faith that millions of professing Christians do not understand. Saving faith must involve a personal commitment to the Lord Jesus Christ as well as an intellectual understanding of who He was and what He did for our salvation.

In John 1:12 we are told, "As many as received Him, to them He gave the right to become children of God."

While it is true that we must intellectually assent to the essentials of the gospel, intellectual assent is not enough. John says that we must "receive" Christ to become a child of God. This truth is symbolized in the following acrostic.

What Is Faith?

Forsaking
All
I
Take
Him

This is why it is so dangerous to tell people, "All you have to do to be saved is to believe that Jesus died for you." Nowhere does the Bible ever use such language. Nowhere does it ever speak of salvation as a simple assent to doctrine. We must receive the Christ of the gospel as well as assent to the facts of the gospel in order to be saved.

Magic Words

Satan will try to instill the idea that salvation is a magical act of man in which if he merely says the right words he will be automatically saved. This is a powerful device of Satan to keep people from being truly born again.

Many years ago I was asked by an evangelist to children to accompany her to the slums of New York City. Since I wanted to see the evangelism she was doing, I agreed.

Within minutes, 25 little children gathered to watch her do a puppet show. When she came to the invitation, she held up a roll of LifeSavers candy and said, "Jesus is the true LifeSaver and He wants to come into your heart. Every child who asks Him to come into his heart will receive a roll of candy. Now, who wants to receive Jesus today?"

Of course, all of the children raised their hands, and she led them in a group prayer. When they were finished, she clapped her hands and squealed with joy and then proceeded to hand out a roll of candy to each child.

On the way back to downtown Manhattan, she rejoiced that all these children were now saved because they had prayed to receive Jesus. She led dozens of such children every week to the Lord.

With heaviness of heart I mentioned that it was likely that most of the children prayed to get the candy and not to receive Christ. She became very angry at what I said and argued that someone is saved the moment he prays to receive Christ. I responded that children can be manipulated to ask Bozo the Clown into their hearts just as easily as Jesus. The "sinner's prayer" is not a magical incantation which mechanically brings about salvation.

Salvation is an act of God and not an act of man (John 1:13). Just saying the right words does not automatically save anyone! We must be saved by Christ through a work of the Holy Spirit.

Do not misunderstand me. I believe in praying to receive Christ just as John 1:12 teaches. But I also believe that people can pray to receive Christ for the wrong reasons as well as for the right reasons. Just praying a prayer never saved anyone.

The Four Soils Parable

The story that the Lord Jesus Christ told in Matthew 13:3-9 is very instructive. He gave us a parable of four different kinds of soils or dirt.

First, there was the hard soil which had been pressed down by people walking on it. When the seed fell on this beaten-down dirt, the birds came and ate it.

Second, there was a kind of soil that was just a thin layer of dirt but underneath was rock. When the seed tried to develop roots, it could not do it. The heat of the sun baked it on that rock and it died.

The third kind of soil was a dirt full of the seeds of thornbushes and weeds. These weeds and thornbushes strangled the plant that tried to grow and killed it.

Finally there was the good ground which had been plowed, prepared, and fertilized. It was the ground that gave fruit unto eternal life.

In verses 19-23, the Lord Jesus explained what the parable meant. The ground that was beaten down represents someone who hears the message of the kingdom but does not understand it. The evil one comes and snatches away what was sown in his heart.

The second soil represents someone who hears the Word, receives it at once with joy, but because there is no root, he lasts only a short time. When trouble or persecution arises because of the Word, he jumps out as quickly as he had jumped in.

The third kind of soil represents someone who heard the Word but the worries of this life and the deceitfulness of wealth choked it and made it unfruitful.

Finally, the good soil represents the man who heard the Word, understood it, and produced fruit in his life.

All four people represented were hearers of the Word. They all claimed to be believers at some point. But three of the four hearers were not truly saved because their hearts had not been prepared to receive the Word. They never produced any fruit. Their profession of faith was an empty profession.

• • •

We've looked at ten very clever devices of Satan, which he uses to keep people from being saved. Be prepared for them and have your answers ready when you meet people who offer these excuses. You may have the opportunity to overcome Satan's devices to lead people into a true and living relationship with Jesus Christ—a relationship without excuses.

Conclusion

We have barely scratched the surface of all the nefarious schemes utilized by the devil and his demonic host. Yet, we have dealt with the popular devices which he is using against individuals, families, churches, and the world today.

We who live at the end of the twentieth century may be witnessing the last ticks of God's prophetic clock. Of all people, Christians must not be asleep while the devil works his dark designs.

The time has come to move forward—not retreat backward. With the armor of God on, the Banner of the Lord above us, and the Captain of our salvation leading us, victory will be ours.

Suggested Reading

Corrie ten Boom, *Defeated Enemies* (Fort Washington, PA: Christian Literature Crusade, 1963).

Thomas Brooks, *Precious Remedies Against Satan's Devices* (Edinburgh: Banner of Truth Trust, 1968).

Demon Possession, John Warwick Montgomery, ed. (Minneapolis: Bethany House Publishers, 1976).

Frederick S. Leahy, *Satan Cast Out* (Edinburgh: Banner of Truth Trust, 1975).

John L. Nevius, *Demon Possession* (Grand Rapids, MI: Baker Book House, 1968).

The Research and Education Foundation is dedicated to investigating those issues which threaten the future of Western culture and the Christian church. For a full listing of available books, audiotapes, and videotapes, contact:

Research and Education Foundation

P.O. Box 141455
Austin, TX 78714
(512) 441-0592

Other Books by
Dr. Robert Morey

The Battle of the Gods
Death and the Afterlife
An Examination of Exclusive Psalmody
Fearing God
Here Is Your God
Horoscopes and the Christian
How to Answer a Jehovah's Witness
How to Answer a Mormon
How to Keep Your Faith While in College
How to Keep Your Kids Drug Free
An Introduction to Defending the Faith
The Islamic Invasion
The New Atheism and the Erosion of Freedom
Reincarnation and Christianity
Studies in the Atonement
The Truth About Masons
When Is It Right to Fight?
Worship Is All of Life